Temp. C.
(Give to John

Related titles from Macmillan Education

Assessment: From Principles to Action
Robin Lloyd-Jones and Elizabeth Bray

Reading: Guides to Assessment in Education
Bridie Raban

Resources for Reading – Does Quality Count?
UKRA Conference Proceedings, 1985: Editor, Betty Root

In Preparation:
Children Becoming Readers
Henry Pearson

Other Macmillan titles by Denis Vincent

New Macmillan Reading Analysis
Effective Reading Tests

Assessing Reading

ASSESSING READING

Proceedings of the UKRA Colloquium on the Testing and Assessment of Reading

Edited by

Denis Vincent, A. K. Pugh and Greg Brooks

MACMILLAN
EDUCATION

First published 1986

Published by
MACMILLAN EDUCATION LTD
Houndmills, Basingstoke, Hampshire RG21 2XS
and London
Companies and representatives
throughout the world

Printed in Hong Kong

ISBN 0–333–41774–7

Contents

The contributors

GREG BROOKS is Senior Research Officer in the Department of Language at the National Foundation for Educational Research, The Mere, Upton Park, Slough SL1 2DQ. He is a member of the Assessment of Perfomance Unit Language Monitoring Project which carries out national surveys of the language performance in English of 11- and 15-year-old pupils in England, Wales and Northern Ireland.

MADELINE LUTJEHARMS teaches German for Special Purposes at the Dutch-speaking Free University of Brussels, Pleinlaan 2, B-1050, Brussels, Belgium. Her research is mainly on the testing and teaching of foreign language reading comprehension.

HELEN MULHOLLAND is a Lecturer in the Centre for Medical Education, The University, Dundee DD1 55Y. Her research interests include the effects of text structure on children's reading and the reading difficulties of older children.

MARY NEVILLE has taught in schools and colleges in several countries and in the Universities of Calgary and Leeds. Her research has been mainly in the area of initial and intermediate reading but recently she directed the national Scottish English Language monitoring programme. This included the performance of primary and secondary school children in oracy as well as literacy. Her address is now University House, 325 Perth Road, Dundee DD2 1LH.

ALASTAIR POLLITT is a Lecturer in Education in Edinburgh University and is Assistant Director of the Godfrey Thomson Unit for Educational Research, 24 Buccleuch Place, Edinburgh EH8 9JT. CAROLYN HUTCHINSON is a Research Associate in the Godfrey Thomson Unit. They have carried out research into several aspects of educational assessment and their current projects include the development of a secondary school English language test battery and various tests of language, maths and reasoning for children aged 7-16.

FRANK POTTER is a Senior Lecturer in Language and Reading at Edge Hill College of Higher Education, St Helens Road, Ormskirk, Lancashire L39 4PQ. He has carried out research into children's use of context in reading. His current research interests include the implications of the New Information Technologies for Literacy and promoting Language as Communication in a variety of media - including newspapers, radio, television, videotext and electronic mail.

TONY PUGH is a Staff Tutor in the School of Education, the Open University, Fairfax House, Merrion Street, Leeds LS2 8JU. His recent research has been mainly into eye movements and head movements in reading. Earlier studies have included cloze procedure, listening while reading, use of books to locate information and reading efficiency of university students. He has also written on the teaching of English, on the history of reading and on the analysis of texts.

PETER PUMFREY is Reader in Education at the Centre for Educational Guidance and Special Needs, Department of Education, University of Manchester, Manchester M13 9PL. His recent research has focussed on the identification and alleviation of children's reading difficulties. Earlier publications have included the affective and cognitive effects of remedial teaching of reading, educational screening, counselling and reading and the dyslexia controversy. A second edition of his UKRA Monograph **Reading: tests and assessment techniques** was published in 1985.

BARRY STIERER is Research Associate in the School of Education, University of Bristol, 22 Berkley Square, Bristol BS8 1HP, where he is a member of the team evaluating the DES Records of Achievement pilot schemes. He has carried out research into the use of volunteer reading helpers in Primary Schools and was a member of the Evaluation of Testing in Schools project at the University of London Institute of Education. His doctoral research was an ethnographic study of reading assessment in primary schools.

GEOFFREY THORNTON was a member of the Schools Council Programme in Linguistics and the Teaching of English and one of the team that produced **Language in Use** and **Exploring Language**. He has been an English Adviser in Cheshire and more recently an English Inspector in the Inner London Education Authority. Since his retirement he has undertaken, for the DES, an appraisal of the APU Language Monitoring Programme. His address is 17 Meadow Walk, Gt Abington, Cambridge CB1 6AZ.

DENIS VINCENT is Reader in Education in the Department of Education and Management in the Public Sector, North East London Polytechnic, Longbridge Road, Dagenham RM8 2AS and was previously a member of the Assessment of Performance Unit Language Monitoring Project. He has worked on a variety of test development projects, including tests of adult literacy, spelling and individual and group reading tests. He has published a number of guides and texts on the testing and assessment of reading. MIKE de la MARE is a Research Fellow in the same department where he is currently working on the development of tests for assessing the progress of remedial readers.

Introduction

Greg Brooks

The ten papers in this volume represent the edited proceedings of a Colloquium on the Testing and Assessment of Reading which took place at North East London Polytechnic in March, 1985. The Colloquium was supported by the United Kingdom Reading Association, and organised by the three editors of this volume.

Because these are the proceedings of a conference, and not a collection of invited chapters on given themes, they do not, or even claim to, represent a 'state of the art' volume: for that see the relevant chapters in Waller and Mackinnon (1979) and Mackinnon and Waller (1981a, 1981b, 1985), and/or the relevant entries in Pearson (1984).

Moreover, this is not a guide to tests and methods of assessment: for that see Pumfrey (1985), Vincent (1985) and Vincent et al. (1983). However, Pumfrey's chapter, does review the instruments available in Britain for assessing pupils' attitudes to reading - a rather different enterprise from assessing reading itself.

Another topic on which little is said, overtly at least, is the why of testing reading. Only Stierer deals with this in any detail, though I hope to show that all the authors share a view of what reading tests should be like, and that this view is informed by a model derived from applied linguistics.

What this volume does contain is reports of (and reflections on) ten different research projects that have recently been completed, or that in some cases are still in progress. Most of the projects, as might be expected, are concerned with tests of (or involving) reading for English-speaking schoolchildren and with how to improve such tests.

A conventional introduction might at this point proceed to describe each of the papers in turn: but I propose instead to describe, briefly, only those papers which do not fall directly within the volume's central focus just mentioned, and then to analyse various themes that seem to run through two or more papers.

The three papers which seem to me to be 'outliers' are those by Pumfrey, Pugh and Lutjeharms. The factor that distinguishes Pumfrey's paper is, as already mentioned, that it deals with tests of attitudes rather than performance: but like all the authors Pumfrey is concerned to show what is lacking in the tests he describes, and what further work needs to be done. Two particularly valuable emphases in his paper are his distinction between cognitive, affective and 'conative' aspects of reading, with his identification of the conative as the most neglected: and his concern for the 'elusive link between attitudes and performance'. As he points out, the Assessment of Performance Unit (APU) surveys - also described in this volume by Thornton - included tests both of reading itself and of attitudes to it, and found a modest but statistically significant correlation between the two, particularly between negative attitudes and low performance. But this is only the beginning of an investigation: what determines these attitudes, and what can be done about them?

Pugh's paper is not directly concerned with any of Pumfrey's three 'psychological' aspects, but with one aspect of the physiology of reading, namely eye-movements and what can be learnt from them about covert, internal reading processes. His findings, though tentative at this stage because of the small numbers of children tested so far, have radical implications for the attempt to deduce psychological processes from physiological data, and to base diagnoses and treatment of reading disability on supposedly 'abnormal' eye-movement patterns. Pugh's data suggest that French and English schoolchildren differ significantly in their pattern of eye-movements and head-movements while reading: this might imply that diagnoses of reading difficulty based on eye-movements should at least take into account the possibility of cultural differences.

His observation that clearer 'reading' eye-movements can be obtained from an eye which cannot possibly be reading - because it is covered - than from the other, which is fixating the print, threatens to undermine the entire logic for inferring reading processes from eye-movements. And even more immediately, especially when linked to other disconfirming research (Newman et al., 1985), it puts a large question mark beside well-intentioned therapeutic programmes which seek to remediate reading difficulties, supposedly caused by unfixed ocular dominance, by covering one eye in the hope that the other will learn to lead (e.g. Stein and Fowler, 1982; cf Times Educational Supplement, 21 June 1985, p.22).

The two factors which distinguish Lutjeharms' research are that it deals with second-language reading of adults, specifically of German by (mainly) Dutch-speaking students. This should serve to remind us that there is far more to the assessment of reading than testing schoolchildren on their first language. (Some parts of the 'universe of possible reading tests' seem, however, to be sparsely occupied: there appear to be few tests of reading specifically designed for children resident in Britain whose mother tongue is not English, for instance.)

3

What may strike a predominantly English-speaking readership as curious about Lutjeharms' paper however, is the need she feels to defend and argue for the use of students' L1 in testing the reading of an L2. Isn't this what goes on most of the time in modern-language teaching anyway? But then Lutjeharms is clearly thinking more of adult groups of learners of any age. But then again it may be as well to be reminded of the 'direct method' possibility (cf. Howatt, 1984), namely that a good approach may be to reduce as far as possible the use of L1 in a foreign-language classroom.

The first of the themes that run across papers has already been mentioned, namely the link between attitudes and performance referred to by Pumfrey and Thornton.

Another is the finding, mentioned by both Mulholland and Thornton, that poorer readers seem to concentrate very heavily on the surface meaning of texts, and therefore have difficulty in detecting irony, etc. While this is clearly important, it is not immediately obvious what can be done in practical terms to help poorer readers with this problem, except perhaps to give them extra practice.

Seen from a different viewpoint, that finding might be seized upon by test-constructors as one relatively easy, and probably valid, way of devising items which will discriminate well, in the statistical sense. Such items would certainly be fairer to testees than those which owe their power to discriminate mainly to what Pollitt and Hutchinson castigate as 'non-reading sources of difficulty', e.g. ambiguity, in exam papers and by implication in test items. An object lesson in just this problem is handled with tact by Potter, whose paper demonstrates the difficulties that can be encountered by highly-motivated teachers seeking to increase the validity of their in-school tests. Other problems in being fair to both

testees and testers, while still producing valid
and reliable tests, are at the heart of Vincent
and de la Mare's paper.

The most important issue I wish to draw
attention to has begun to emerge in the last
paragraph, namely the validity of reading tests.
The feeling that word-recognition and sentence-
completion tests have had their day has grown in
strength and acceptance for at least the last ten
years. Such tests tap only very superficial
aspects of reading, and are invalid because they
do not even attempt to reflect the diversity and
range of text types, and reading purposes, which
real readers experience outside the confines of
traditional tests. Even if such tests correlate
very highly with better tests (as Stierer says),
and even if better tests are more expensive and
time-consuming, the old tests must still be
rejected because of their low validity, and their
detrimental backwash effect on teaching.

It is probably accurate to claim that the first
project (in Britain at least) which attempted to
follow the logic of this argument through, and
actually produce more valid tests, was the APU
Language Monitoring Project at the National
Foundation for Educational Research in England
and Wales, of which Vincent was a member in the
early days (1977-79) and on which Thornton
reports. The APU tests (for details of which see
the references under 'APU' at the end of
Thornton's paper) were based on whole texts,
produced in small book form, with an accompanying
answer booklet, and were designed to provide real
- or realistic (cf. Thornton) - reading tasks,
both literary and 'factual'.

Stierer rightly points out that the first APU
surveys did also use one of the old, invalid,
sentence-completion tests, the NS6. However, it
may also be appropriate to point out that this was
done only in the first year of a five-year
programme of annual monitoring, at the insistence

5

of the Steering Group, and solely to provide a 'statistical link' (supposing anyone should need to use it) with the previous series of roughly four-yearly national surveys of reading dating back to 1948.

The influence of the APU approach to reading tests, or perhaps more accurately of the linguistic thinking behind it, is now spreading quite widely. Neville's survey in Scotland was committed to the same principle, though in that case again the Edinburgh Reading Tests were included for comparative purposes. Similarly, Lutjeharms uses full texts (newspaper articles). Pollitt and Hutchinson are also following the logic of this principle in a full battery of language tests which they are developing (see Hutchinson and Pollitt, 1985). And a small book plus answer booklet format has been adopted by Vincent and de la Mare (in press) for a series of group reading comprehension tests for junior schools.

It is only by adopting such a policy that anything approaching an adequate sampling can be taken of the range and variety of texts that readers might encounter for their multifarious purposes. Such an approach might also begin to end the long-running arguments about what Neville archly calls 'the same old thing - comprehension'. Disputes about the single or multiple nature of comprehension are pointless without specifications of text types and readers' purposes, and may seem still more pointless when we have convincing specifications of both those domains.

Meanwhile, we have to struggle with the more mundane problems, pointed out by Stierer, of inadequate resources and conservatism which need to be overcome before any 'new wave' of tests can achieve widespread acceptance and use. Whatever their faults, the old tests are both cheaper and less time-consuming, and more familiar to teachers. Moreover, as Root (1985) pointed out, better reading schemes have not necessarily always driven out worse ones: so how can it be expected that better reading tests will necessarily drive out worse ones? While there is a market for the old tests, most publishers will continue to print them.

How might publishers be persuaded to replace older-type tests with more enlightened materials? In Britain, by and large it is teachers who order and use tests, but Local Education Authorities who pay for them. One might hope that teachers will switch of their own accord to the new tests, but this is probably naive. Change will require action on the part of LEAs, such as issuing lists of tests which they will, and more importantly will not, pay for: perhaps some already operate such a policy. It would be given much more force however, if the Department of Education and Science (DES) were to lend its name to two such lists. Is this too much to expect?

This might represent an undesirable move towards centralisation of control of the education system - but there seem to be several other straws in that particular wind at the moment (not the least the importance the DES seems to be attaching to the dissemination of APU findings from all its monitoring projects, not just language). This particular piece of central control might attract the support of those best qualified to judge the issue, and still fail to be implemented because of opposition from those who object in principle to all centralisation.

Yet, that objection would conceal a further paradox. One of the less desirable trends in the testing of reading in recent years has been the growth of blanket testing of whole age-cohorts within LEA areas by the LEAs themselves, using on the whole the older, invalid tests I have been criticising. This too represents a form of centralised control, if not at national level,

7

which may have effects on classrooms which are not wholly desirable. LEAs could not validly object, in these circumstances, to being told by a higher authority to put their house in order.

Let us suppose that my fantasy of a prohibition on worn-out tests came true. There would be a remarkable convergence of principle and pragmatics: the principle that new tests should replace old ones, and the practical reality that LEAs would no longer be able to afford blanket testing, because the new wave of tests do take more time to administer and also simply cost more. Then, the new tests would have to be used more discriminatingly, and for more acceptable purposes, such as diagnosis of reading problems and the monitoring of overall levels of performance by light sampling.

The constructors and publishers of tests would also then have more incentive to fill in gaps in the existing panoply. One such gap I have already identified, namely the lack of tests for second-language speakers of English. Another is the lack of a properly normed measure of the reading ability of students in further or higher education. Much of the research on the psychological processes in reading is conducted with undergraduate subjects: yet the reading levels of the subjects are very rarely reported, even when they are divided in some way into 'better' and 'poorer' readers (both highly relative terms at this level). Even when they are reported, they are based on unstandardised measures of restricted generalisability.

These are just two of the directions which developments in reading tests might take next. And it is heartening to conclude by noting that they can be tackled whether my pipedream about the death of the old tests is realised or not.

References

Howatt, A.P.R. (1984) A History of English Language Teaching. Oxford: Oxford University Press.

Hutchinson, C. and Pollitt, A. (1985) Background to the English Language Skills Profile. Occasional paper, Godfrey Thomson Unit, University of Edinburgh.

Mackinnon, A.R. and Waller, T.G. (Eds.) (1981a) Reading Research: advances in theory and practice, volume 2. New York: Academic Press.

Mackinnon, A.R. and Waller, T.G. (Eds.) (1981b) Reading Research: advances in theory and practice, volume 3. New York: Academic Press.

Newman, S., Karle, H., Wadsworth, J.F., Archer, R., Hockly, R. and Rogers, P. (1985) Ocular dominance, reading and spelling: a reassessment of a measure associated with specific reading difficulties. Journal of Research in Reading, 8 (2) 127-138.

Pearson, P.D. (Ed.) (1984) Handbook of Reading Research. New York: Longman USA.

Pumfrey, P.D. (1985) Reading: tests and assessment techniques, (2nd edition) Sevenoaks: Hodder and Stoughton.

Root, B. (1985) President's opening address. United Kingdom Reading Association Annual Conference, University of Reading, July 1985.

Stein, J.F. and Fowler, S. (1982) Diagnosis of 'dyslexia' by means of a new indicator of eye dominance. British Journal of Opthalmology, 66, 332-336.

Vincent, D. (1985) Reading Tests in the Classroom: an introduction. Windsor: NFER-Nelson.

Vincent, D., Green, L., Francis, J. and Powney, J.
(1983) A Review of Reading Tests. Windsor: NFER-
Nelson.

Vincent, D. and de la Mare, M. (in press) The
Effective Reading Tests, Levels 1-4. Basingstoke: Macmillan.

Waller, T.G. and Mackinnon, A.R. (1979) Reading
Research: advances in theory and practice, volume
1. New York: Academic Press.

The Scottish National Assessment of Reading: An Integrated Language Approach

Mary Neville

For the past two and a half years, I have been directing a testing programme which may be used in the future to monitor the English language capabilities of Scottish school children. 'Directing' is really too grand a word since our 'team' consists of Sheila Kydd, my research assistant, Fiona Keyte, our secretary, and me. Thus we are all involved in a great variety of tasks and our job descriptions change dramatically from month to month. For the first three months of the project, I worked on my own looking generally at the feasibility of assessing English language in a large-scale testing programme, and I produced a preliminary report which put forward some specific proposals for types of tests and batteries of tests that might be used in the testing programme.

We had a few major hurdles to overcome. To begin with, our timetable allowed no room for extensive or protracted pilot testing or, indeed, for much reworking of any part of the programme. After my feasibility study, we had just 15 months to develop our tests, set up our sample, produce our material in bulk and send it out to the schools. After the one month allowed for testing, we then had a further 15 months to analyse the results and write and produce our report. Perhaps this kind of timing would not have worried a group of people organized for large-scale survey testing of the population, but I had been accustomed to testing smaller groups. The Scottish Education Department statistical

11

adviser thought that a sample of about 6,000 would be best for the present project. That required quite complicated administrative procedures, especially when setting up the sample and dealing with the test materials.

Apart from timing and the size of the sample, a further problem was the ages of the children to be tested. In the past, the Scottish Education Department (SED) had conducted surveys of reading ability at Primary 4 and Primary 7 (that is, ages 8-9 and 11-12) using the **Edinburgh Reading Tests**. They wanted me to test these stages again, not only for purposes of comparison, but also because these are important milestones in primary education. Primary 4 children should have achieved basic literacy; Primary 7 marks the end of primary education.

The SED also considered that Secondary 2 (ages 13-14) is another important stage, since it ends the period of general, non-examination-type education; thereafter, children move into the final stages of their secondary education where the national examinations and more formalised school assessments presumably measure progress. So, I had to produce tests suitable for three age groups, each comprising about 2,000 children.

The reading tests

Of course, I had adequate funds to buy **Edinburgh Reading Tests** and send these around to a random sample of children in our sample of 330 schools (stratified by size and region). However, these days, such an approach would be altogether too simple-minded. Although the Edinburgh tests are made up of subtests which are supposed to measure different subskills of reading, Lunzer and Gardner (1979), amongst others, have shown that all the subtests are highly interrelated and all seem to measure the same old thing - comprehension (however we may define that). The **Edinburgh Reading Tests** do the job of measuring general comprehension well but they are quite expensive for schools to buy, and take rather long to administer. Although the tests are well known and used in Scotland fairly widely for administrative purposes, the SED felt that other methods of assessing such a general ability as reading comprehension should be examined. We suggested cloze tests as an alternative. Among the headteachers, the advisers and the inspector who 'steered' us there was also the strong feeling that some study skills in reading were not adequately tested by the Edinburgh tests. So we had a clear directive to produce some more reading tests to broaden the base of the testing of reading in Scotland.

Luckily, Tony Pugh and I had been working for a number of years in Leeds on 'Ability to Use a Book' (Neville and Pugh, 1975 and 1982) and, in Aberdeen, Fyfe and Mitchell (1983) were well advanced in their examination of the assessment of dictionary skills and in their study of the formative assessment of reading generally. At the same time, near Edinburgh, Mulholland (1984 and this volume) was working on cloze tests. So, without too much waste of time, we were able to adapt the excellent materials already available in Scotland so that they could be administered by teachers as tests to groups of children.

When Mulholland first began work on her cloze tests, she developed them for use with normal readers aged 9-10, and for poor or remedial readers aged 12-13. However, she found that even older, normal and good readers still made many errors in the tests and she decided that the tests could be used for a wide range of reading ages (and chronological ages).

Of course, as Hutchinson and Pollitt (1985) say, we cannot 'protect' children from the English language and present to them material that will be truly suitable only for one stage. Knowledge of English language in oral or written form is not, like most other areas of the curriculum, under the control of the teacher. Children of any age have easy access, in and out of school, to an enormous range of language, particularly when they are able to read, and it seemed to me that, with our timetable, we might have great difficulty in grading our reading tests reliably. Apart from this difficulty, however, the range of reading ability is of interest in itself. I was keen to see whether that range at P4 would overlap with the range at P7 or even at S2. The only way to make these kinds of comparisons, and also to avoid mistakes in grading of difficulty, was to try, as far as possible, to give the same reading tests to all our sample from age 8 to 14.

This we did. However, in our Dictionary Test we did need to have an easier dictionary for the young children, even though the types of subtest overlapped between P4 and P7/S2. The Study Skills Test was the same except for the subtest of ability to use the index and table of contents. In this subtest, the younger children answered only the easier, first half of the questions. The cloze tests, not surprisingly, were exactly the same for P4, P7 and S2.

Listening, writing and speaking tests

Added to the problem of our three stages was our biggest difficulty. Our brief was to try to test English language and also to set up a feasible language monitoring programme for the future. The area for testing and/or monitoring was language, not reading. Now, I knew a bit about testing reading and I had even dabbled in testing listening (Neville, 1967a and 1975). Tony Pugh and I had also compared the performance of children on cloze tests of reading and listening (Neville and Pugh, 1974 and 1976). However, now to be added to the testing of listening and reading was also the testing of writing and speaking.

This is not the place to describe in detail our batteries of listening, writing and speaking tests. I need only to say that in each language mode we had three or four major tests, each of which we hoped would test different skills at each mode; these major tests were made up of between two and five subtests. In some areas, such as spelling, punctuation and vocabulary for the younger, P4 children, we either shortened the tests or used four subtests graded in difficulty; the P4 children took the first three, and the P7/S2 the last three subtests. Otherwise, at each stage, the tests were the same, apart from a somewhat different format for the test papers for the younger children. To round off the test package, Sheila Kydd developed attitude tests of Writing, Speaking and Listening. These were modelled on the **Attitude to Reading Tests** already developed in Dundee by Ewing and Johnstone (1981). Attitude tests were included to give some 'affective' information which might have value for teachers and curriculum planners part-icularly in the area of oracy which is, at present, being seriously considered in secondary school assessment programmes. The four attitude tests were, however, administered only to the Tayside schools in our sample, since we wanted to interview some of the children who took those tests.

It must be obvious that we had to simplify our approach as much as possible to enable our programme to go forward on time. We did this in two ways. First, as I have explained, we used the same tests at all stages whenever possible. Second, we tried to use the same tests, or at least the same stimulus material, in two or even three modes. Thus, we used the cloze tests also as listening cloze tests; we used a writing task also as a speaking task (and with the same marking scheme). This speaking task, as well as three others, gave us the transcripts on which to base our listening tasks. This approach also enabled us to make extremely interesting comparisons, not only across stages but also across modes.

15

The integrated test

While we were devising our reading and listening tests, I was anxious to make sure that we had both 'product' and 'process' measures of these receptive skills (Johnstone, 1981). Our cloze tests were, of course, process measures but we were obliged to use products or answers to questions for some of our other tests. As much as possible, we asked for answers that merely involved ticks, crosses, drawing routes on a map, drawing a diagram and the like but, at times, children had to listen to, or read, a question and write a short answer. I have, for some time been concerned over the number of intervening agents who come between the reader and writer of a text when we measure comprehension. I wondered whether we could not do better with our product measure than only follow the same old comprehension-question approach with question setters and question markers acting at times like confounding factors. One method that we thought would be worth a try was the free recall method (with probe questions).

Any discussion of this problem of measuring a receptive language skill leads one immediately to the interdependence of the various modes of the 'language act', as it was rather simply depicted in the 1960s and 1970s. A further simplification of this model is given in Figure 1 and it does show

Figure 1: Model of the Language Act

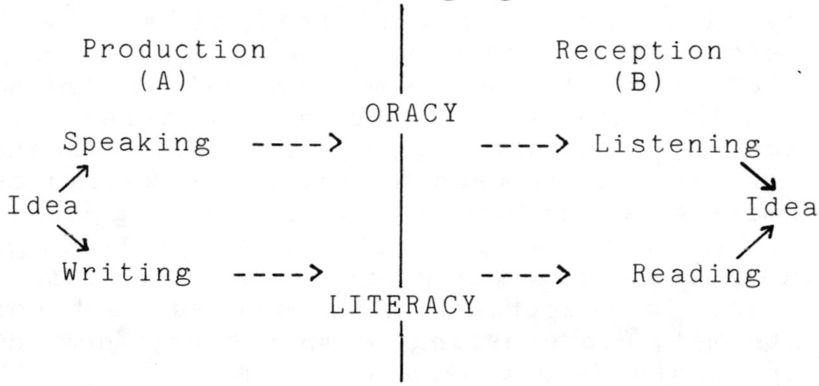

the parts played by the producer (A) and the receiver (B), whether or not they choose to use the route of oracy or of literacy.

Of course, the division between oracy and literacy can become blurred when vocalisation enters the scene but we are not concerned here with that complication. In Figure 2, a second assessment section has been added, and there the role of 'production' in the assessment of reading or listening is clearly seen.

Figure 2: Model of Assessment of Modes in the Language Act

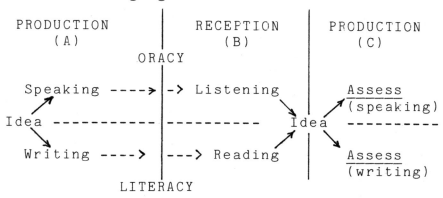

As I pondered on this and, at the same time, thought of our problems of range of difficulty of the test materials, plus our need to test in the four language modes, I considered whether it would not be possible to add a certain elegance to our economical testing programme. Rather than just give groups of differing tests for any one mode (albeit 'converting' tests in one mode for use in the other modes) surely we could simply use one piece of stimulus material to provide measures of ability in all parts of the language act: reading, listening, writing and speaking. Figure 3 shows that the product produced by B will then not only measure how well B received and understood the message (and idea) emanating from A, but that same product can also be assessed for its value purely as a product.

Figure 3: Model of Unified Assessment of the
         Language Act

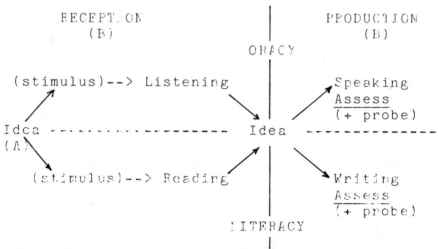

Well, this idea is simple enough. Our problem now
was how to turn it into a test which could be
administered reliably to hundreds of children at
three different ages by the teachers in many
different schools.

Constructing the test

It should be clear to the reader who has followed
my careful written cues that we intended to use
free recall with probe questions as measures of
comprehension (reading and listening). A number
of people have used this method quite
successfully (e.g. Meyer and McConkie, 1973;
Brown and Smiley, 1977). In fact, when working
with young children, I had used Piaget's method of
parcelling out main ideas in a fairy story to
measure how many facts a child retold to a partner
(Neville, 1967b) and I thought we could use a
similar approach with our test.

First, we had to choose our stimulus material.
For a narrative piece of writing, obviously a folk
tale would be the best because such material is
suited to all ages, and we were lucky enough to
find a short, clearly written folk tale from the

Western Isles about a swan maiden (Colwell, 1975). For comparative purposes, I wanted also to have a piece of informative writing and here it was more difficult to find something suited to all ages. Finally, we took a passage on keeping rats and mice as pets from the book which Tony Pugh and I had used with small groups of 9- to 10-year-old children in Leeds (Silverstein and Silverstein, 1968). The readability measure gave a reading age about 9:6 for this passage, and only about 8:6 for the Swan Maiden, but any easier informative text seemed to be babyish in style. Although all the children tested were presented with the Swan Maiden in its entirety (655 words in length), we gave a shorter section of Rats and Mice to P4 (645 words), compared to an excerpt of 1,043 words for P7/S2.

Next, we abstracted the main ideas of each passage. For the Swan Maiden and for the P4 Rats and Mice passage, there were 13 of these; the longer Rats and Mice passage had 20 main ideas. We then made up a corresponding probe question for each main idea. Finally, the passages and probe questions were printed and also recorded on tape for replaying on tape recorders in the schools. While preparing our stimulus material, we had also been wrestling with the practical problem of how to conduct our speaking tests. In the end, we had decided to make extensive use of the micro-cassette recorders that businessmen use to record their memos and letters in aeroplanes and trains. So, armed with two of these, Mrs Kydd and I set off to pilot-test our Integrated Test at P4 and P7 in a most accommodating nearby Tayside primary school. To our amazement, the test administration seemed to be remarkably smooth. We listened for groans and gasps of horror from the children and looked for other less obvious signs of dismay, especially at P4, but they all seemed to find the tests perfectly straightforward and apparently not unlike the tasks that their own teachers asked them to do.

Administration of the tests

For reading, the actual administration was of the following pattern. The children were told that they would read a story about the Swan Maiden (or keeping rats and mice as pets) and that they would have to write down the story for children in P2 to read. Because, we said, some of these young children cannot yet read very well, two or three children would not write the story but would record it on tape for the young children to listen to. Thus, we hoped to give the children a realistic reason for their work. The children were told that the reading would be timed (five minutes for the Swan Maiden and nine minutes for Rats and Mice). They were also warned that, after their writing or speaking they would have some questions to answer about their reading. Since we allowed 25 minutes maximum for the writing/speaking, we estimated that all parts of the test could be completed within an hour.

And so it proved to be. The children started to read but, after two minutes (four minutes for Rats and Mice) were told to stop for a moment and put a cross on the word they were just reading (for a later check of reading rate). Then they were told to continue for the allotted time (re-reading was allowed if children finished before the maximum time). Writing of the story and recounting on tape proceeded simultaneously; we found that three children from the group could retell with time to spare during the 25 minutes allowed to the rest of the group for writing. To help the speakers remember what they had read until their turn to recount arrived, we asked them to design a cover for the story booklets that the other children were writing, and I must say that we received some really splendid pictures. Of course, it was necessary to have another teacher or auxiliary worker either to supervise the writers and the speakers not actually recording, or to tape the speakers. At the end of the writing/speaking session, the children came together as a group and were given the probe questions to answer. That completed the test.

Listening followed exactly the same pattern except that the stimulus material was heard on tape and later the probe questions were also heard on tape (though the children wrote their answers to these oral questions). There was, of course, no test of speed of listening.

We tried out our test once more with S2 children to make sure that some hardened 14-year-old children did not reject our Swan Maiden or that the more nervous and susceptible of our sample did not express horror at the notion of keeping rats and mice as pets. When this did not happen, we were ready to try out the test with teachers as test administrators. This was really the acid test because any researcher can try out his/her own ideas and, somehow, make them 'work'. I tried to keep the instructions as simple as possible and I sent only a reading or a listening mode package to any one class. There was one P4 and one P7 class involved in each of two different schools. We asked the teachers to comment on anything in the tests that seemed to them to be causing problems of any kind whatsoever and, of course, there were difficulties. But they were really minor and we found that we were getting back from the schools plenty of usable test results.

The national testing

Our final sample consisted of groups of 20 randomly chosen children in 25 schools at each of our three stages. At each stage, these 25 schools were chosen randomly from amongst the 100+ schools of our total school sample. In each school, 10 children were assigned randomly to the reading or listening mode of the test. Within this group of 10, we chose arbitrarily three children to be the speakers. At each mode, children read or listened first to the Swan Maiden and then to Rats and Mice. Obviously this was a complicated and initially rather confusing testing pattern for the teachers to follow. It was also time-consuming for the teachers, the more so since they were also asked to carry out other speaking tests. It says a good deal for the resilience of the teachers that nearly all the schools carried out the testing and did it so carefully that, out of more than 2,400 tests received back from the schools, only about 30 were spoilt (and most of those came from one school where the teacher administering the test was ill). What pleased us especially was that the recorded 'stories' were clear and we could score them as readily as we could score the writing.

Marking the tests

The marking scheme gave us nearly as many problems as constructing the test. Picking out the main ideas from the writing or the speaking was not difficult. Marking the probe questions was not a problem either, and a final comprehension mark could be arrived at which was made up of the main ideas plus any additional main ideas subsequently given via the probe questions. What was more difficult was deciding how to score for details which were the same as those in the stimulus passages, and also how to give credit for flights of fancy (we called it elaboration) that went outside the text but still contributed to the worth of the written or spoken story. Finally, we marked details from the text quantitatively and we added this mark to the main idea-plus-probe score. This composite mark was then our comprehension score (either for listening or reading). Writing and speaking had a quantitative content component of main ideas plus detail, but to this were added scores for the qualitative categories of elaboration, logical development, and language and style. This marking was rather complex at first but it was carried out chiefly by two markers. Mrs Kydd and I checked very carefully all their work and also marked about a quarter of the tests ourselves. We double-marked some tests, and here the inter-marker reliability was 0.86 for comprehension and 0.77 for the total writing and speaking scores. But, with larger groups of markers, this extent of agreement might be difficult to maintain for the writing and speaking scores.

Analysing the results

After the pilot testing, we used the computer to carry out some statistical tests of our data from P4 and P7. You may recall that, for the final pilot test, we had used complete classes within a school (i.e. P4 or P7) for reading or listening modes of the test. We did find some mode differences between stages when we performed analyses of variance for these factors. We found that P4 children performed better after listening to the passages than after reading them. Both their comprehension and their writing and speaking were better. This mode difference was not found for P7. All the P4 and P7 children performed less well on the informative than on the narrative test material and, for the narrative material, the P7 children did better than the P4 on all the tests. However, P4 children who listened to ' Rats and Mice' performed, in their writing, as well as P7 children (whether or not they had read or listened). Of course, there were high correlation coefficients between performance of the two types of passage and also between such 'subtests' as reading rate and main ideas. However, the relationships between the probe scores and other measures of comprehension were less straight-forward and suggested different patterns of recall for narrative and informative tests.

What of our major testing programme and the analysis of the data? About 1,200 children performed the tests (each child doing both narrative and informative tests) and for each test there have been entered in the computer file either 18 or 20 separate scores for each child (i.e. about 45,000 entries). Because of the structure of the sample and the structure of the test we are able to perform analyses of variance using the mode and stage as factors. We can also compare the narrative and informative scores in various ways and look for sex differences by stage, by mode, and by text-type for our various subtest scores. Interrelationships between the text types and the various subtests can also be studied.

All this information is just becoming available to us and will still require some time to digest fully. One thing, however, is clear from this large sample where the listening and reading modes were tested within the same class or stage in a school: between modes there is no clear mode difference at any stage for comprehension. That is, the better listening, compared to reading, found in our P4 pilot 'listening only' class (from a school in a fairly 'good' catchment area), has not been found with our large representative sample of schools and with a split-mode testing programme carried out in a single stage in each school. The writing scores for P4 are also lower than those of P7 (and S2). As we listened to tapes and read stories and then perused the associated probe questions time and again we were amazed to find that not only 'readers' but also 'listeners' seemed to have missed vital parts of the plot of the narrative (and even more of the facts given in Rats and Mice) or to have listened to only parts of the story. Yet, when we administered the tests ourselves we could have sworn that we had the total attention of at least our listening group. This disconcerting result we have found not only with the primary school children but, to a surprising extent, amongst our secondary sample. Possibly the work of experimental psychologists on the effect of the regular abstract structure of folktales on their recall and reconstruction (Bower, 1976) may help us explain our findings. The work relating theories of text processing and text structure to learning from texts will also be helpful (Mandl, Stein and Trabasso, 1984).

24

Conclusion

After a rather innovative testing programme such as this, we have to ask the question, 'Would we do it again the same way?'. For our Integrated Test the answer is 'Yes'. So much lip-service has been paid, and still is paid, to the notion of the interrelationships of the four modes of language that it seems a good idea to try to capitalize on this interrelationship for measurement purposes. The next time, however, we would probably try to lighten the burden of testing for the teachers (e.g. perhaps give either narrative or informative tests within the same school, although still in the two modes of reading and listening).

The teachers themselves gave positive reactions to the tests except for two or three P4 teachers who felt that the retelling aspect of the tests was too hard for their slower pupils; no teacher objected to the levels of difficulty of the stimulus texts. The tests seemed, perhaps, not unlike real school work, yet were, at the same time, so structured that very interesting comparisons could be made easily between the receptive modes and also between the productive modes.

Using two types of text was interesting, too. There is no doubt that the teachers, especially in the secondary schools, were amazed at the inept performance of some of their pupils, particularly after reading or listening to the passage on Rats and Mice. With other children, fluent writing or speaking could mask the lack of content which the probe questions showed was due to poor comprehension. The purpose for reading (or listening) and writing/speaking in the test seemed to be convincing; much of the work that we received was in a most appropriate register.

In future testing, our Integrated Test could not really serve as a single 'portmanteau' test for all modes. In reading, we would also need to look at study skills, although we could, perhaps, ally this to an informative stimulus text. But a single test is probably too short to give an adequate picture of the level of functioning on a national level. Nonetheless, for a teacher wanting information on a class, or comparisons for diagnostic purposes, as well as for the educational administrator trying to find out quickly about levels of ability, such a composite, snapshot type of test has much to commend it. Moreover, the idea is quite simple and teachers (or test constructors) can easily choose their own stimulus material and then use it, as we did, to test comprehension of reading or of listening, and production of writing or of the spoken word. What, to me, was surprising was that we could use the same test material over such a wide age range and that we could, so to speak, animate our Figure 3 to the extent of receiving back from all over Scotland, properly completed test papers and tapes from which we could then produce usable test data.

Our final results, including the results of our reading and other language mode tests, will be presented in our 1985 report to the Scottish Education Department. These results will enable us to describe and compare the language abilities of Scottish school children at three important stages of their education.

References

Bower, G.H. (1976) Experiments on story understanding and recall. Quarterly Journal of Experimental Psychology, 28, 511-534.

Brown, A.L. and Smiley, S.S. (1977) Rating the importance of prose passages: a problem of metacognitive development. Child Development, 48, 1-8.

Colwell, E. (1975) Tales from the Islands. London: Kestrel Books, Penguin Books, 85-88.

Ewing J. and Johnstone, M. (1981) Attitudes to Reading. Dundee: Dundee College of Education.

Fyfe, R. and Mitchell, E. (1983) Formative Assessment of Reading Strategies in Secondary Schools. Report to the Scottish Education Department. Aberdeen College of Education.

Hutchinson, C. and Pollitt, A. (1985) Background to the English Language Skills Profile. Occasional Paper, Godfrey Thomson Unit, University of Edinburgh.

Johnson, P. (1981) Implications of Basic Research for the Assessment of Reading Competence. Technical Report No. 206, Center for the Study of Reading, Urbana-Champaign: University of Illinois.

Lunzer, E. and Gardner, K. (Eds.) (1979) The Effective Use of Reading. London: Heinemann Educational for the Schools Council.

Mandl, H. Stein, N.L. and Trabasso, T. (1984) (Eds.) Learning and Comprehension of Text. Hillsdale, N.J.: Erlbaum.

Meyer, J.F. and McConkie, G.W. (1973) What is recalled after hearing a passage? Journal of Educational Psychology, 65, 109-120.

Mulholland, H. (1984) The Interaction with Text of Failing and Normal Readers. Unpublished Ph.D. Thesis, The Open University.

Neville, M.H. (1967a) Factors affecting listening comprehension. Alberta Journal of Educational Research, 13, 201-209.

Neville, M.H. (1967b) Understanding between children of the same age. Alberta Journal of Educational Research, 13, 221-229.

Neville, M.H. (1975) Effectiveness of rate of aural message on reading and listening. Educational Research, 18, 37-43.

Neville, M.H. and Pugh, A.K. (1974) Context in reading and listening: a comparison of children's errors in cloze tests. British Journal of Educational Psychology, 44, 224-232.

Neville, M.H. and Pugh, A.K. (1975) Reading ability and ability to use a book: a study of middle school children. Reading, 9, 23-31.

Neville, M.H. and Pugh, A.K. (1976) Context in reading and listening: variations in approach to cloze tasks. Reading Research Quarterly, 12 (1) 13-31.

Neville, M.H. and Pugh, A.K. (1982) Towards Independent Reading. London: Heinemann Educational.

Silverstein. A. and Silverstein, V. (1968) Rats and Mice: friends and foes of man. Glasgow: Blackie, 65-70.

The APU and the Assessment of Reading

Geoffrey Thornton

The Assessment of Performance Unit (APU) was set up within the Department of Education and Science (DES), by the government of the time in the mid-seventies. In October 1975, the Unit set up a working group to consider what forms assessment of language performance might take, and draw up specifications for those who were to develop the actual means of assessment. The thinking of that group was summarised in a pamphlet called **Language Performance** (DES, 1978).

The Language Monitoring Team had by then begun its work, based at the National Foundation for Educational Research (NFER). The first assessments, of reading and writing, were carried out in 1979, with pupils aged 11 and 15. In all, five annual assessments have been done, with oracy being added to reading and writing in 1982, after a two-year research and development period. Some 47,000 primary and 45,000 secondary pupils have taken part in the surveys.

The results have been published in a series of reports with the general title **Language Performance in Schools** (APU, 1981, 1982a, 1982b, 1983, 1984a, 1984b, in press), and discussed further in pamphlets by members of the team (Brooks, 1985; Gorman, 1985; MacLure and Hargreaves, 1985; White, 1985).

The APU approach

The Bullock Report (DES, 1975) argued in Chapter

3, 'Monitoring', that 'an entirely new approach' to the assessment of reading was needed. To replace the existing, very narrow tests, it recommended that forms of assessment should be developed based upon a definition of literacy 'capable of showing whether the reading and writing abilities of children are adequate to the demands made upon them in school, and likely to face them in adult life. ... we are suggesting that monitoring should be extended beyond the limit of a single dimension to give more information than has ever been available before'.

In the 1982 Primary survey report (APU 1984a) the APU Language Monitoring Team summarised the concerns underlying the development of their reading test materials. They were:

1. A concern to represent a wide range of reading materials, appropriate to the age-group, drawn from the educational context and from outside school.

2. A concern to present reading, even in a test situation, as a meaningful activity, so that the texts used are either complete in themselves or have a thematic or conceptual coherence.

3. A concern to make the tasks set appropriate to the material, in relation to the original context of the writing. The use of the word 'task' rather than 'question' denotes the fact that pupils were asked to respond to texts in different ways, such as note-taking, annotating, strategies such as underlining, completion of tables and diagrams, extended written responses and discussion.

4. A concern to reflect the natural interrelationship of the different modes of language use, reading, writing, speaking and listening.

Reading Booklets were designed to put materials in front of the 11- and 15-year olds selected to take part in the surveys. The contents of the booklets fell, broadly, into three categories - works of reference, materials encountered for practical purposes in daily life, and literature.

The booklets based upon reference materials contained selections of thematically related reading, with a contents page, an index, and page or chapter headings to provide the sort of cue normally encountered when consulting works of reference. Booklets also included charts, diagrams, tables and maps. The extracts were organised to form a coherent whole, containing many of the features of reference books, and arranged in such a way as to expose readers to information of greater detail and complexity as they read through the booklet.

Booklets containing materials that pupils might encounter outside school included extracts from comics and magazines; forms to be filled in; sets of instructions; notices; signs and labels; lists of various kinds, and a travel brochure.

The literature booklets contained pieces complete in themselves, such as short stories or poems, or extracts of autobiographical writing from different sources. In reply to suggestions that works of literature should not have been included in the tests the leader of the team concludes in his report on the assessment framework (Gorman, 1985), 'In our view, the abilities required to interpret language used for literary or aesthetic purposes do not differ in any fundamental way from those needed to interpret language used for other purposes. All intelligent reading involves the creative interpretation of "words on the page" ... Nor is it assumed that "literary language" differs in any radical way from language used for other purposes. All literate pupils are assumed to be capable of understanding and appreciating some aspects of works of literature, provided an appropriate selection of such materials is made'.

The questions put to pupils, or the tasks they were asked to complete, through the medium of the booklets, differed in terms of their forms, their scope and the reading strategies involved and the type of responses required.

Differences in form relate to aspects of the meaning that has to be derived from what is read, while the scope of a question related to the amount of material that has to be read in order to answer it. Form and scope largely determine the reading strategies that have to be adopted, for example, the careful word-by-word reading required for poetry, or the rapid scanning needed in other cases.

In addition to written responses, those taking the tests were asked to complete forms, fill in posters, label diagrams, or make notes. The guiding principle in devising questions was that they should be questions likely to be asked by an experienced teacher. Ways were also devised of eliciting attitudes to reading, in the belief that, as the 1982 *Primary Survey Report* (APU, 1984a) has it, 'The crux of learning to read is the independent use made by pupils of their reading skills. Such use will depend on pupils' opinions and feelings about the usefulness and value of reading skills, and the perceptions of their own abilities in relation to these skills'.

Information was sought on pupils' main motives for reading, and the purposes to which they put it; types of reading preferred; use of library resources, and preferences with regard to those classroom activities involving talking or writing about books read; and attitudes towards reading aloud, or independent reading. The reading surveys have thus yielded a large amount of data, providing evidence of reading performance at 11 and 15, and information about the ways in which pupils see themselves, and their abilities, as readers; about why they read, what they read and when and where they like to read.

It is widely believed, on the basis of previous research, that there is a correlation between attitude and performance. The APU surveys indicated a consistent but low correlation between the two, with negative attitudes particularly correlated with poor performance. While it is not always true to say that a positive attitude produces a good performance, it is often the case that negative attitude is accompanied by poor attainment.

Reading in primary schools

The 1982 **Primary Survey Report** (APU, 1984a) says that 'Relatively few children of eleven in the sample appeared to have problems with actually decoding the printed word, but it is equally clear that many are not yet fully competent readers'. Given this, the question which it seems appropriate to ask about the children's reading is not, 'Can they read?', or even 'What can they read?' but, 'What sort of sense are they making of what they read?'. Eleven-year-olds bring to their reading a bundle of preconceptions and assumptions based upon past experience. In this, they are no different from any other readers, of whatever age and experience. The assumptions and perceptions brought to reading do not differ, either, from those brought to any other problems that life presents. The (necessarily) limited experience of 11-year-olds, however, means that the way in which they approach a text may not always match the demands it is making upon their skill as readers. This argues the need for as wide as possible a range of reading experiences, described as a 'repertoire' in the report.

It is to be hoped that, whatever their experiences, it will have given them a positive attitude. Their attitude, whatever it is, will derive from a view of reading as an activity, of what it involves, of the satisfaction (if any) to be obtained from it, together with a view of their own ability as a reader. The view of reading prevalent in the home, and the opportunity for reading that exists there, must be significant ingredients. So, more directly, must the view projected by teachers, explicitly in comment or implicitly through tasks set; the conditions provided for reading in the classroom or school; and the point of them as perceived by the pupils. Their success, or otherwise, in tackling reading tasks will determine what view they have of their own ability and so condition the attitude with which they approach further tasks.

'Reading necessarily involves a process of formulating hypotheses.' Successful reading requires the formulation of appropriate hypotheses. 'It is characteristic of poor readers that while they quite certainly form hypotheses, are active readers, and make some sort of sense in relation to what they read, they do not appear to be consistently alert to the need to revise their "readings" and to monitor their own interpretation against the text' (APU 1984a). Difficulties arise from the mismatch between the children's preconceptions of what the text requires and the nature of the text itself, and if they have no strategies for closing the gap these difficulties will not be overcome. In the chapter devoted to Primary Reading in the Team's review of the five-year monitoring programme (APU, in preparation), the opportunity is taken to look in some detail at what differentiates the responses of high and low scorers to certain tasks.

Low scorers often based their responses not on the text in front of them but on some pre-existing personal knowledge which influenced their approach. They exhibited a marked reluctance to modify initial perceptions, to the extent that interpretations incompatible with those perceptions were virtually excluded. Those who scored highly, however, revealed themselves willing, and able, to adapt initial assumptions to take account of new information in the text. Low scorers demonstrated an inability to pick out relevant clues from the text, other than a key word which might lead to a correct answer. They tended to rely upon invention rather than deduction, on inappropriate quotation from the text rather than appropriate inference. High scorers on the other hand, displayed greater versatility, and were more successful at selecting and re-ordering relevant facts from a text into a synthesis of their own.

The formulation of these differences in terms of high and low scorers underlines the fact that all readers, no matter what their reading ability, may from time to time encounter difficulties with unfamiliar texts, and emphasises one very significant finding of the APU Language Surveys, namely that pupil response was crucially related to the nature of, and the demands made by, particular tasks. Response is task-specific.

This points to the conclusion that classrooms, expecially in the formative years of Primary School, should be places which not only offer pupils wide experiences of reading, but places which encourage them to engage actively with texts, supported by teachers and class-mates. Work on texts requiring active collaboration between pairs or small groups of pupils, and between pupils and adults (not always necessarily the teacher) is valuable in showing how 'to consider the range of meaning that can be derived from a written text, and the context, educational or social, that makes one interpretation more legitimate than another'. Many of the tasks in the surveys required responses involving underlining or annotating, and the reorganisation of the text to make or complete, tables and diagrams. Activities like this, which force the reader to question the text, and an initial interpretation of it, are likely to assist a final interpretation. For those learning how to come to terms with texts, supportive activities of that kind demonstrate how it is possible to devise strategies which will lead to their becoming confident and independent readers.

The Attitude Questionnaires revealed, among eleven-year-olds, an ability to discriminate between liking to read and needing to read, with emphasis on the former. They also revealed a willingness to read for pleasure, especially at home, where you can read when you want to, not when somebody tells you, and where you can be sure that nobody will ask you to read out loud or write about what you have read. Both these latter activities attracted significant expressions of dislike. This is not necessarily to argue that pupils should never be asked to write about what they have read, but that the practice of routinely requiring a few lines about each book read is likely to diminish the pleasure of reading. If, on the other hand, books are discussed, with reasons for liking or disliking articulated as a prelude to a review, perhaps in a publication for next year's Top Juniors, then a number of advantages accrue. There is an audience, there is discussion, there may be drafting and proof-reading - activities that provide insight into the writing process.

Reading in secondary schools

The surveys produced evidence that there is, in secondary schools, a narrow view of reading, of the purposes for which we read, and of the potential of reading in the learning process. The point is made in Chapter 3, 'The Study of Attitudes to Reading', in the 1979 Secondary Survey Report (APU, 1982b). 'It was noticeable in responses to the open-ended questions that "reading" was perceived by pupils as predominantly connected with activities in English lessons, and principally with fiction

36

reading'. It is noted that 'This interpretation tallies with the findings reported in a recent Schools Council study, (Lunzer and Gardner, 1979) that the majority of time devoted to continuous reading in the secondary schools studied was in English lessons, while the use of reference and library sources was limited in the other subjects studied, and "in most lessons reading for learning seems to have a relatively junior role"'. The chapter concludes, 'the tenor of our findings accords with the general decline in enthusiasm towards reading from age 11 noted by HM Inspectorate (in Aspects of Secondary Education in England, HMI, 1979), and raises many of the same questions about the range and purpose of the reading at school of 15-year-old pupils and its relationship to pupils' voluntary reading for personal satisfaction through the extension of knowledge or enjoyment'.

The surveys also revealed important differences between the performance of boys and girls at both primary and secondary levels. Girls not only performed better, but they revealed more positive attitudes towards reading. By the age of 11, boys have begun to develop more negative attitudes towards reading than girls, and this correlates with poorer performance. The Secondary Surveys revealed a similar picture. Girls expressed more pleasure at reading for self-improvement, and a more positive attitude to school activities connected with reading. There is a correlation between performance and attitude, which suggests that positive action must be taken to overcome boys' reluctance to read, not only in English but also in those subjects which depend on reading for the acquisition of knowledge.

Much of the reading done in English will be of literature. It was considered essential to include literary works in the surveys because, as 'the Bullock Report claimed, there is a sense in which literature brings the pupil 'into an encounter with language in its most complex and varied forms'. Nevertheless, as has been emphasised, 'the capacities required to interpret language used for literary or aesthetic purposes do not differ in any fundamental way from those needed to interpret language for other purposes'. All reading requires the interpretation of the information given by the writer, the making of inferences, the construction of meaning, the understanding of what may be implied rather than explicitly stated. In literature, the clues provided for the reader may be more subtle. The differences between the approaches of those pupils who scored highly on their responses to the short stories they were asked to read, and those who scored poorly, highlight the difficulties experienced by poor readers, and suggest the kind of help they need.

Those who scored highly were able to interpret the stories as integrated pieces, with the elements seen as relating to the whole. Their sense of form enabled then to see the overall structure of the story and the pattern within, and they were seemingly able to hold in their minds a number of options so that they could modify interpretations when more information became available. Poorer readers, on the other hand, tended, having made a judgement, to maintain it, even when the evidence accumulated against it. This may be related to a lack of confidence, a reluctance to move beyond a position in which they felt, albeit wrongly, a sense of security.

The other area in which those who scored poorly showed weakness was in their inability to move beyond a literal interpretation of the text. They found it hard to realise that what was said did not always correspond with what was meant. Uses of metaphor, irony, and symbolism were not always understood, resulting in failure to discern underlying themes or to grasp a writer's viewpoint. Reading responsively, questioning the text, using one's own experience to interpret it, are, as Bullock pointed out, necessary ingredients of reading intelligently. This should be kept in mind when considering approaches to reading in the classroom. In particular, the value of presenting pupils with short extracts, followed by questions, as in traditional 'comprehension exercises', might be examined. It is of great importance not only that the type of task given to pupils should be productive, but that the view of language, and of underlying linguistic processes, transmitted by the exercise should be reconcilable with an adequate linguistic model.

In the 1982 Secondary Survey Report (APU, 1984b) it is recorded that a majority of pupils find some enjoyment in reading, and in writing. If this is indeed the case, then there is at least a foundation of interest to build on. In their answers to the questionnaire, pupils consistently indicated an association between enjoyment, performance and their perceptions of themselves as readers. English Departments should place self-perception high on the list of qualities to be encouraged as they seek to provide for their pupils a range of reading experiences that could be regarded as adequate in the terms suggested by the surveys.

References

APU (1981) Language Performance in Schools: Primary Survey Report No. 1. London: HMSO.

APU (1982a) Language Performance in Schools: Primary Survey Report No. 2. London: HMSO.

APU (1982b) Language Performance in Schools: Secondary Survey Report No. 1. London: HMSO.

APU (1983) Language Performance in Schools: Secondary Survey Report No. 2. London: HMSO.

APU (1984a) Language Performance in Schools: 1982 Primary Survey Report. London: DES.

APU (1984b) Language Performance in Schools: 1982 Secondary Survey Report. London: DES.

APU (in preparation) Language Performance in Schools: A Review of Language Monitoring 1979-1983. London: DES.

Brooks, G. (1985) Speaking and Listening: assessment at age 15. Windsor: NFER-Nelson.

DES (1975) A Language for Life (The Bullock Report). London: HMSO.

DES (1978) Language Performance. London: DES.

Gorman, T.P. (1985) The Framework for the Assessment of Language. Windsor: NFER-Nelson.

HMI (1979) Aspects of Secondary Education in England. London: HMSO.

Lunzer, E. and Gardner, K. (1979) The Effective Use of Reading. London: Heinemann for the Schools Council.

Maclure, M. and Hargreaves, M. (1985) Speaking and Listening: assessment at age 11. London: DES.

White, J. (1985) The Assessment of Writing: pupils aged 11 and 15. Windsor: NFER-Nelson.

The Validity of Reading Comprehension Tests: What Makes Questions Difficult?

Alistair Pollitt and Carolyn Hutchinson

'And so it is, Oh Lord, I measure it.
But what it is I measure
I do not know.'

St Augustine: 'Confessions'

Some questions are more difficult than others.
This may seem rather an unnecessary observation
to make, but it does point to a very curious
historical feature of educational and psychological research - very few people have ever asked
'Why?'. The contention of this paper is that
educational assessors would profit greatly, both
practically and theoretically, from studies
aimed at answering the question 'What makes our
questions difficult?'

The rationale for such studies, and the
justification for calling them construct validation studies will be explained first, and then
the process of validation will be illustrated by
current work on reading comprehension in
certificate examinations being carried out in the
Godfrey Thomson Unit.

The study of question difficulty

Our investigation began with a project supported
by the Scottish Education Department and the
Scottish Examination Board. We set out to
identify and characterise 'difficult' questions
from past Scottish O Grade papers in English,
French, Geography, Chemistry and Mathematics, in

41

order to provide assistance for question setters devising papers for the new Standard Grade system, and especially for the Credit (most difficult) level within it. The results of the project, indicating features of questions, both subject-specific and general, that cause difficulty for 16 year-olds, and the implications that we see for the assessment and indeed the concept of attainment are described elsewhere (Pollitt et al., 1985; Entwistle and Hutchinson, 1985). Only a few points will be considered here.

The approach was to seek those features of questions which seemed to cause or remove difficulty in questions, irrespective of whether these features seemed intentional or unintentional, valid or invalid. The questions were divided into 'easy' and 'difficult'; candidates' written responses to the 'difficult' ones (most of the questions were of course not objective) were scrutinised to find out what mistakes they made. From these we inferred the causes of difficulty, and checked these inferences by comparing the difficult questions with the easy ones. To a limited extent it was possible to quantify these ideas; then the research plan became to identify those features that increase or decrease the facility value (or difficulty index) of questions in a predictable way and to quantify each feature's contribution.

It was possible to pursue quantification furthest in the study of reading comprehension. An explicit model of the process of answering questions about a passage was developed and hence an explicit equation enabling us to predict, from features of the questions and their interactions with the text, the difficulty of each question. This explicit model, in addition to its usefulness in the writing of reading test questions, also has the considerable attraction to researchers of offering an empirical means of testing and comparing - and of falsifying - alternative theories as to what really is measured by tests.

42

Studies of published objective tests in the United States led to a formation of ideas very similar to these in what was called 'A Theory of Construct Definition', by Stenner et al. (1983). They argue that the most important task in educational or psychological measurement is the process of ascribing meaning to the scores produced by measurement procedures, and this process must depend on an understanding of the procedure, or an explanation for the observed patterns in the data. They stress the essential symmetry of test data (Rasch, 1960; Wright and Stone, 1979), in that every response available for analysis arises from the meeting between a person and a question, and specify six conditions that must be met before a score can be interpreted validly. A 'construct theory' consists of a response model (such as the Rasch model) to predict the outcome of such meetings, and four explicit equations explaining question difficulties, person scores, question discrimination and person 'discriminability' (or item and person fit). Then, if the measurement is precise enough for the purpose at hand, individual scores can be interpreted and the test has construct validity.

The main difference between our approach and that of Stenner and his colleagues is in the extent to which causal theory should be incorporated in construct definition. The American approach is strongly empirical, concerned with finding question characteristics that maximise the predictive power of the model, and so runs a risk of imputing causation to mere correlations. We believe that the choice of characteristics to be included and the way in which they are to be used in the study should both be guided by an explicit model of the answering process.

Common to both research groups are a concern to achieve a better understanding of the construct measured by the test, and a belief that the study of variation in question difficulty is the most promising way to seek such an understanding. Why is such an emphasis placed on the construct and the questions?

Many different kinds of test validity have been proposed, each implying its own procedures for collecting evidence that the test is indeed providing the information that the user is seeking. The differences between the various definitions are often quite subtle or even superficial and most can be classified into the three main groupings of criterion, content and construct validities. It has been fashionable for some years to refuse to speak of the validity of a test, but only of the validity of a test use. In this view it is not the measurements that are valid or invalid but the decisions taken as a result of the measuring process, and this validity is estimated empirically by comparing the measurements obtained to an established criterion measure. Such criterion validation is essentially empirical and utilitarian. But it is also ad hoc and anti-theoretical, since each new use of the test requires a new validation exercise, and no accumulation of knowledge about the test is possible. It has also been common in recent years to distinguish educational tests from psychological tests by stressing their dependence on content validation procedures, arising from a precise specification of the subject elements and processes (domains) to be included in the various sections of the test. Such careful control of test content by prior specifications is indeed a necessary part of the production of any good educational test, but it is wholly a subjective procedure with no empirical basis in test data. Indeed content validity has been denigrated as merely a sophisticated version of face validity, where a test is called valid merely because a group of self-styled experts think it is. Only construct validity of the three main types combines a theoretical perspective and hence the possibility of a growing understanding of the construct, with an empirical approach to the investigation of that theory.

Construct validation (including concurrent validation as a simple case) has traditionally involved the analysis of variation in person scores, usually by investigating the correlations between children's test scores and their scores on other tests or on measures of social background or educational experience. But there are several reasons for advocating a greater emphasis on question scores, the other side of the symmetrical data set.

1. Question scores are more reliable than person scores. When tests are being investigated there are usually many more people than questions since several hundreds or even thousands of children may be given the same test of 50 or 60 questions. This means that facility values or difficulty indices are normally estimated with much more precision than are candidates' scores.

2. Questions are more amenable than persons. There are no ethical problems in probing those characteristics of questions that might be relevant to the construct. Furthermore, the questions are public and open to study by any interested investigator, and constant in that they do not change with time and so remain available for the testing of hypotheses not yet proposed involving characteristics not yet considered.

3. Questions can be altered and manipulated at will. Rigorous experimental designs can be applied to the testing of different versions of a question in order to confirm or refute hypotheses about factors affecting difficulty. The problems of sampling and experimental controls in education apply to people, not to questions.

4. Question scores are of central concern in test construction. Test theory has concerned itself mainly with the interpretation of test results, and the help provided to the test constructor has almost exclusively been

concerned with maximising the reliability of test scores. Validity can be built into the construction process by using an explicit construct theory model to predict question difficulty before trials take place. Sometimes post hoc validation may not be possible; with certificate examinations even question trials and item analysis may not be possible. In such cases, only the theory-driven prior control of question difficulty can hold out much hope for the improving of validity.

5. A test is a set of questions not of people. If we wish to validate a test it seems more obvious to seek to understand the behaviour of its questions rather than the behaviour of some people. Test constructors can reasonably be expected to know their questions, and may reasonably be challenged to explain why one question is more difficult than another. If they cannot answer, can they really claim to understand what they are measuring?

A Validation Study of O Grade Reading Comprehension

In the project described earlier it was possible to identify four main areas in which errors occurred in reading comprehension tests.

1. In READING the question rubric and understanding the task.

2. In SEARCHING the text in order to find the correct piece or pieces of text from which the answer could be derived.

3. In UNDERSTANDING the meaning of these text pieces, either at the level of decoding or of interpreting.

4. In COMPOSING an adequate written response.

It was also found that these broad areas covering the process of answering a question were dependent each upon the next, so that the process could be seen as a sequential one, at any point of which a candidate might both drop marks and lose any chance of completing the rest of the task successfully.

A more detailed analysis and classification of the errors within the areas described above led to the identification of a number of characteristics of questions and text which could be seen as either 'supports' or 'hurdles' for candidates as they worked through questions. Figures 1 to 5 illustrate a detailed sequential schema for the path the candidate may be assumed to follow in answering each question. The possible sources of difficulty are expressed in the diagrams as questions requiring a yes/no answer. Where 'yes' constitutes a hurdle, the question is marked -; where 'yes' constitutes a support, it is marked +.

At this stage the model was only partly based on evidence. The points of potential influence on difficulty were suggested by the results of the analysis of errors, but their arrangements as a sequential schema with branches and loops is plausible rather than proven. The role of such a model is heuristic; it is a device for organising the later stages of the investigation. Specifically, its primary role is to suggest a (fairly) exhaustive list of characteristics of questions and their interactions with each other and with the text; these characteristics became the variables in the statistical analysis. This particular model was designed to encompass all reading comprehension tests involving a text followed by questions requiring written answers, the type so widely used in secondary school examinations. In particular it includes tests where the text is in a second language, and the questions in either the first or the second language, and our early work with it used questions from both French and English examinations. A model for multiple-choice reading tests would differ from this in some major respects because of the influence of the alternatives offered on the answering process; a model for cloze testing would be very different.

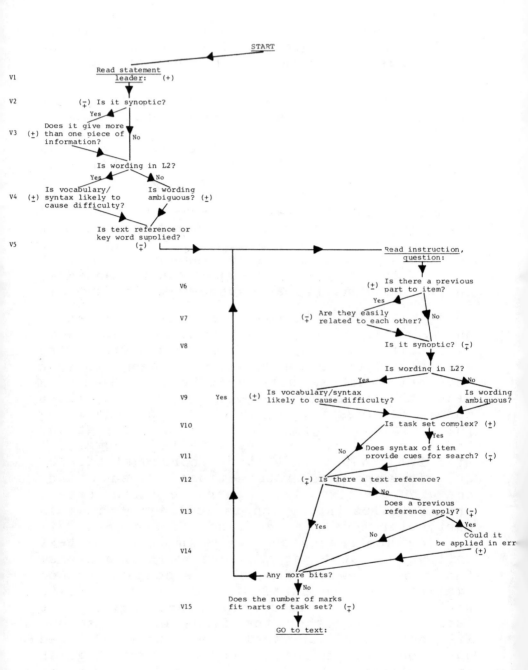

START

V1 — Read statement leader: (+)

V2 — (∓) Is it synoptic?
Yes

V3 — (±) Does it give more than one piece of information?
No

Is wording in L2?
Yes / No

V4 — (±) Is vocabulary/syntax likely to cause difficulty?

Is wording ambiguous? (±)

V5 — Is text reference or key word supplied? (∓)

Read instruction, question:

V6 — (±) Is there a previous part to item?
Yes / No

V7 — (∓) Are they easily related to each other?

V8 — Is it synoptic? (∓)

Is wording in L2?
Yes / No

V9 — Yes (±) Is vocabulary/syntax likely to cause difficulty?

Is wording ambiguous?

V10 — Is task set complex? (±)
Yes

V11 — No Does syntax of item provide cues for search? (∓)

V12 — (∓) Is there a text reference?
No

V13 — Does a previous reference apply? (∓)
Yes / No
Yes

Could it be applied in err (±)

V14 — No

Any more bits?
No

V15 — Does the number of marks fit parts of task set? (∓)

GO to text:

Figure 1: Reading the question

48

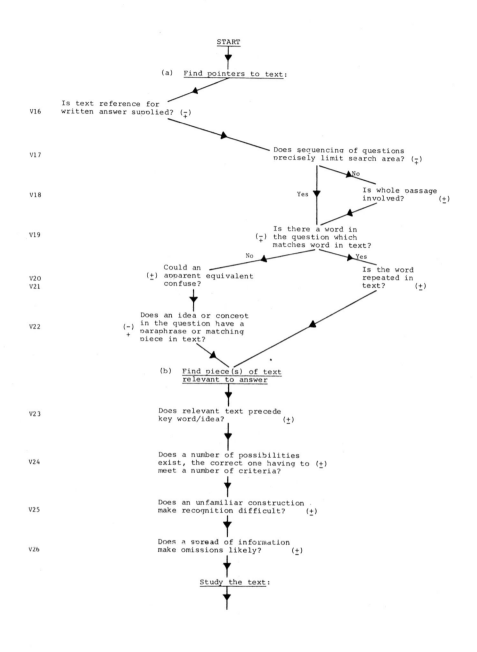

START

(a) Find pointers to text:

V16 — Is text reference for written answer supplied? ($\frac{-}{+}$)

V17 — Does sequencing of questions precisely limit search area? ($\frac{-}{+}$)

No

V18 — Is whole passage involved? ($\pm$)

Yes

V19 — ($\frac{-}{+}$) Is there a word in the question which matches word in text?

No   Yes

V20 — Could an apparent equivalent confuse? ($\pm$)

V21 — Is the word repeated in text? ($\pm$)

V22 — ($\frac{(-)}{+}$) Does an idea or concept in the question have a paraphrase or matching piece in text?

(b) Find piece(s) of text relevant to answer

V23 — Does relevant text precede key word/idea? ($\pm$)

V24 — Does a number of possibilities exist, the correct one having to meet a number of criteria? ($\pm$)

V25 — Does an unfamiliar construction make recognition difficult? ($\pm$)

V26 — Does a spread of information make omissions likely? ($\pm$)

Study the text:

Figure 2: Searching the text

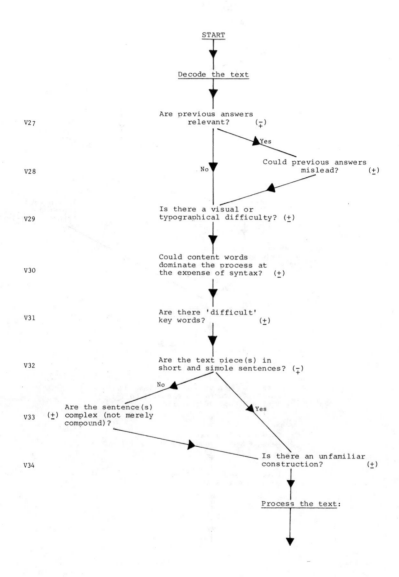

START

Decode the text

V27 Are previous answers relevant? $(\frac{-}{+})$

Yes

V28 No Could previous answers mislead? $(\pm)$

V29 Is there a visual or typographical difficulty? $(\pm)$

V30 Could content words dominate the process at the expense of syntax? $(\pm)$

V31 Are there 'difficult' key words? $(\pm)$

V32 Are the text piece(s) in short and simple sentences? $(\frac{-}{+})$

No

V33 $(\pm)$ Are the sentence(s) complex (not merely compound)? Yes

V34 Is there an unfamiliar construction? $(\pm)$

Process the text:

Figure 3: Interpreting the text (decoding)

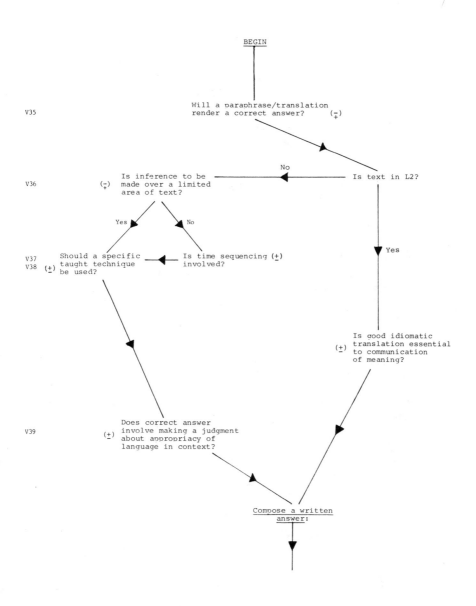

BEGIN

V35   Will a paraphrase/translation
render a correct answer? $(\frac{-}{+})$

V36 $(\frac{-}{+})$ Is inference to be   No   Is text in L2?
made over a limited
area of text?

Yes   No

V37
V38 $(\frac{+}{-})$ Should a specific   Is time sequencing $(\pm)$
taught technique   involved?
be used?

                   Yes

                        Is good idiomatic
                $(\pm)$ translation essential
                        to communication
                        of meaning?

V39 $(\pm)$ Does correct answer
involve making a judgment
about appropriacy of
language in context?

                     Compose a written
                        answer:

Figure 4: Interpreting the text (processing)

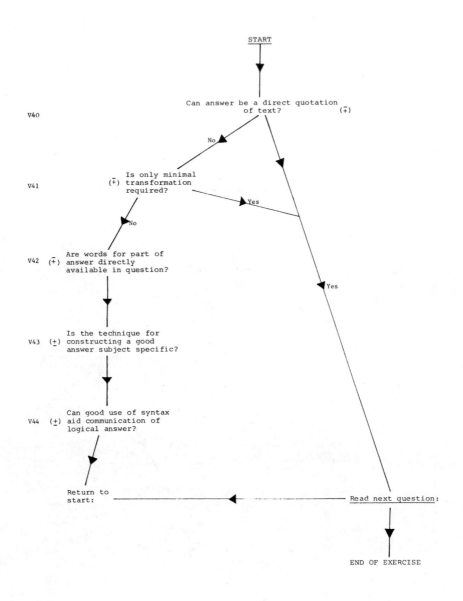

Figure 5: Composing an answer

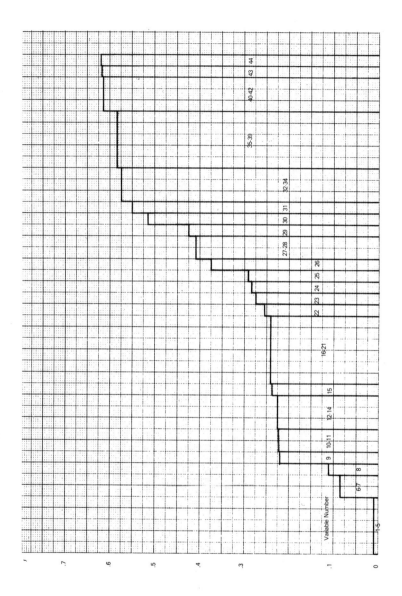

Figure 6: Proportion of variance of difficulty explained by 22 variables

(Figures 1 to 6 are reproduced from Pollitt et al. 1985, What Makes Exam Questions Difficult? by kind permission of the Scottish Academic Press)

But in each case, a more or less sequential model could be proposed as a means of generating and organising the variables.

The aim is to predict the difficulty of questions. For this the appropriate technique is multiple regression. Thus, the sequential nature of the model becomes a crucial advantage. The principal problem in multiple regression studies is deciding how to judge the relative importance of different variables; the apparent importance of one variable may change dramatically if certain other variables are included or excluded. The sequential model offers an answer to this problem. Each variable is added in turn, in strict chronological sequence, and the increase in the model's power to predict difficulty is noted (Cohen, 1968). A variable may correlate quite highly with difficulty on its own, but its value in a model like this depends on its ability to add extra predictive power over and above that already provided by the variables that precede it.

Initial analyses suggested that some of the variables should be grouped together. The first main analysis, therefore, used 22 variables, each of which was one of the original 44 variables or the simple sum of some of them. The growth in R^2 as the model unfolds is depicted in Figure 6. The statistical results are summarised in Figure 7.

R^2 is the square of the multiple correlation coefficient between question difficulty and the set of variables so far; this indicates the proportion of the variation in question difficulty that can be explained or predicted by these question characteristics. The whole set of 22 variables is able to account for 62 per cent of the variation in difficulty, but of course, some of this success, with so many variables, is due to chance effects. The increase in R^2 at each stage can be tested for statistical significance; for the most successful variables the level of significance is indicated.

54

Figure 7

Stage	Variable	R2	Increase	Significance Level
Reading	V1-5	.00	.00	
	V6-7	.09	.08	**
	V8	.11	.02	
	V9	.22	.11	***
	V10-11	.22	.00	
	V12-14	.22	.00	
	V15	.24	.02	
Searching	V16-21	.24	.00	
	V22	.25	.01	
	V23	.26	.00	
	V24	.28	.02	
	V25	.28	.00	
	V26	.38	.09	***
Understanding	V27-28	.41	.04	*
	V29	.43	.02	
	V30	.52	.09	***
	V31	.55	.03	**
	V32-34	.57	.02	*
	V35-39	.58	.00	
Composing	V40-42	.02	.04	**
	V43	.02	.00	
	V44	.02	.00	

*** = $p < 0.01$ ** = $p < 0.05$ * = $p < 0.10$

Expressing these eight variables in order of importance, we can give a first description of the construct measured by these reading comprehension tests. Children scoring well on the tests are those who can cope with difficult questions, and questions are difficult when:

V9   the question wording is potentially ambiguous;

V30   the relevant text contains content words - verbs, nouns, adjectives, especially those denoting attitudes or emotions - which tend to dominate functional details;

V26   the information required for an answer is spread out in the text;

V6-7   there are two or more parts to a question
and they are related to each other in anything other than a very simple way;

V40-42   writing the answer requires more than simply quoting from, or minimally transforming, the text;

V31   the answer depends on knowing a different word;

V27-28   previous answers are relevant, and any earlier errors may mislead;

V32-34   the sentence structure of the text is complex.

Is this a description of reading ability as we would like to construe it? The most important predictor of difficulty seems to be the presence or absence of ambiguity in the question, and the complex interaction of question parts is fourth most important: these have little to do with reading ability - at least as far as the text is concerned. Also significant is the interaction of answers, where a wrong answer in one question may lead to lost marks in later ones: two penalties for one mistake. All of these may be considered as invalid sources of difficulty. It appears that, rather too often, question setters are setting tasks that are intrinsically within the capabilities of most children and are then raising the difficulty level in order to challenge the more able candidates by embedding the task in a complex and misinterpretable question. The ability to understand the text is in danger of being transformed into the ability to disentangle the question and to anticipate the implicit demands of the mark scheme. If the only effect of this research were to make question setters aware of the crucial importance of writing unambiguous questions that clearly set out the task that is required, then it would have made a major contribution to educational assessment.

Another major determinant of difficulty is part of the process of composing the answer. Some questions do not allow the candidates merely to use the language supplied in the text, but require them to produce their own words and structure. This requirement adds a significant amount of difficulty even for candidates who have found the right pieces of text and thoroughly understand them. Markers, and mark schemes, may still penalise candidates for poor expression of their answers, for using inappropriate 'synonyms' or making linguistic errors. This is surely an assessment of writing, rather than reading, and the persistence of this variable, even in fairly good questions, must surely suggest that more objective forms of indicating answers be sought for assessing reading in public examinations.

The other four of the principal variables do seem valid. Successful candidates are those who can avoid being distracted from the real meaning by dominant or emotive words, who can synthesise answers from separate pieces of text and who can cope with difficult words and syntax. These surely are the kinds of abilities we want a reading test to measure.

Further work has suggested some changes to this general model. The process model in Figures 1 to 5 has been refined a little, but the only new 'source' of difficulty which we feel obliged to add is something to allow for the effect of time pressure in an examination, since questions at the end of a paper seem consistently more difficult than predicted by our regression model.

A reconfiguration of the 'READING the question' part (Figure 1) so as to suppress distinctions between statement leaders and questions, did raise one other variable to a more prominent position. When questions are synoptic, in that the wording provides the candidate with some information, usually interpreting or summarising part of the text, the question is made easier. An example of this would be: 'The first eight lines of the passage deal with the same single general topic - stress. Why ...?'

The importance of this variable is the opportunity that 'synopsis' offers the setter for the deliberate control of difficulty. Intrinsically difficult tasks may be brought within the capabilities of less competent children by the planned use of supports like this. Indeed, to generalise for a moment, the use of supports in this way can be seen as equivalent to a definition of attainment; where tasks have clear outcomes, a child's level of attainment may be described by reporting how much help or support he or she needs to complete it.

One impressive feature of the model is its success in dealing with both first and second language papers. Although the data we have studied so far are not conclusive, there is a general agreement between the relative importance of these difficulty sources in English and French examinations. There are, however, some differences. English questions seem less influenced by knowledge of vocabulary, or by misleading effects of earlier wrong answers, neither of which is very surprising. But ambiguity, distracting words, the spread of information, and sentence complexity remain important. And one variable not in the eight above looks as if it may be of very great importance in English tests. Where a question is worth two or more marks, and is either explicitly or implicitly divided into two or more parts, it is not always obvious (to the candidate at least) how the marks will be awarded, and so how fully each part should be treated. Once again, they are forced to guess at the setter's intentions and the markers' expectations. The variable might be termed 'ambiguous criteria'. Its relative importance in English tests seems again to stem from the greater complexity of tasks and questions, and it clearly is again a threat to validity.

There are some significant omissions from the set of ten variables so far described, and two sets are worth particular mention. First, almost nothing in the part of the model dealing with SEARCHING the text makes any contribution to explaining difficulty. Surely, some features to do with textual structure or coherence, or the use of key words or explicit text references, should be important? The fact is that in all of the comprehension tests studied, the order of the questions methodically followed the text. Apart from the few questions at the end of the English tests that reviewed the text more extensively, the order was entirely predictable. The relevant piece of text for the next question was almost always the next sentence or two. Explicit text references were common, but were in practice redundant, and searching skills or the perception of text structure was almost never necessary. But on the rare occasion when a question was out of sequence, or the relevant text piece came immediately before, rather than after, a key word or reference, then the effect on difficulty was, of course, dramatic.

Also missing was any indication that questions requiring inferential skills might be more difficult than those in which the answer was explicitly stated, but here the explanation is quite different. The key variable here should be V35 in Figure 4 - 'Will a paraphrase render a correct answer?' In terms of raw correlations, this variable came second only to 'ambiguity' as a predictor of difficulty, yet when its turn came in the regression analysis, it was not able to increase the prediction significantly. Its ability to predict difficulty is weakened by the presence of other, earlier variables that correlate highly with it. In particular, the need to infer meaning seems to be correlated with the need to disentangle complex or ambiguous questions, since the questions demanding inference very often were themselves expressed in complex or ambiguous language. The high raw correlation of 'inference needed' suggests that this may prove to be an important part of the Reading Comprehension construct if we can screen out the hurdles of doubtful validity.

Further analyses of the same kind are in progress to explore more the role of question characteristics in this type of reading test. We are now able, however, to exploit further the explicitness of the construct definition model by experimental studies in which some features of questions are deliberately modified and the consequent effects on difficulty examined. In one Godfrey Thomson Unit project, the English Language Skills (TELS) Profile is being developed with this approach to validity very much in mind. Questions in Listening, Reading and Writing sections will be written at two or more levels by varying the supports and hurdles (we hope to exclude most of the invalid ones, of course), and item analysis will include, for Reading at least, a test of each variant's fit to the prediction model. Only if we feel able to explain the difficulty of a question will it be allowed to remain in the test.

Our aim is to combine explicit theory with empirical confirmation; not theory about reading but theory about reading assessment. It is the congruence between what a reading test tests, and what we think it should test, that constitutes validity. What does a test really test? We believe the questions can supply the answer.

References

Cohen, J. (1968) Multiple regression as a general data-analytic system. **Psychological Bulletin**, 70, 426-43.

Entwistle, N.J. and Hutchinson, C.J. (1985) Question difficulty and the concept of attainment. In N.J. Entwistle (Ed.) **New Directions in Educational Psychology**, 1. London: The Falmer Press.

Pollitt, A., Hutchinson, C.J., Entwistle, N.J., and De Luca, C. (1985) What Makes Exam Questions Difficult? Edinburgh: Scottish Academic Press.

Rasch, G. (196) Probabilistic Models for Some Intelligence and Attainment Tests. Danmarks Paedagogiske Institut. (Reprinted 1980, Chicago: University of Chicago Press.)

Stenner, A.J., Smith, M. and Burdick, D.S. (1983) Toward a theory of construct definition. **Journal of Educational Measurement**, 20, 305-17.

Wright, B.D. and Stone, M.H. (1979) Best Test Design. Chicago: MESA Press.

Developing a New Individual Reading Test

Denis Vincent and Mike de la Mare

Testing occupies a central position in the Reading Rogues' Gallery, together with phonics and work-books. To qualify for inclusion in the Gallery a practice or approach should be prone either to over-use, mis-use or mis-interpretation. In defence of phonics for example, Morris (1984) has argued for more enlightened 'linguistics-informed' approaches. Testing may ultimately defy such redemption but in this chapter we propose to comment on the largely unexplored topic of 'good practice' in testing.

Our comments arise from the experience of a reading test development project sponsored by Macmillan Education Ltd. During this work we encountered problems which probably reflect intrinsic difficulties in 'testing' reading. We also became aware that little is known about the history of testing in reading and that in spite of a valuable study by Gipps et al. (1983) insufficient is yet known about current or recent trends in the use of reading tests. It is our contention that the availability of better information could enhance the reading tests of the future.

What sort of reading test?

An early decision for any reading test constructor concerns the general form the test is to take. This will be closely linked to the perceived need for a new test in the first place.

Our project was commissioned to produce a series of standardised group tests of reading comprehension and to develop an individual test of oral reading and comprehension. This discussion will deal largely with the latter test for which the aim was not so much innovation as to provide existing test users with an up-to-date alternative to a currently used version.

The complete test, published as the **New Macmillan Reading Analysis** (NMRA) (Vincent and de la Mare, 1985), consists of three equivalent Forms (A, B and C). Each contains six test passages of increasing length and difficulty. These are printed in a single Reading Booklet and each passage is accompanied by a set of comprehension questions to be answered after oral reading. Normative scores are obtained for oral reading accuracy and comprehension and the test manual outlines a number of procedures for carrying out qualitative analysis of a reader's performance. Record Sheets containing the text of the passages are available for recording test performance and summarising results. This format for individual testing is well-established in published materials such as the **Neale Analysis of Reading Ability** (Neale, 1966) and the **Durrell Analysis of Reading Difficulty** (Durrell, 1955).

As publishers of the Neale test, Macmillan aimed to meet the continuing demand for an individual test of oral reading and comprehension. However, it became apparent that little was known about the nature of this demand beyond the fact of its existence. There have certainly been investigations into patterns and practice of testing at national and Local Education Authority (LEA) level (e.g. Bullock - DES 1975; Gipps and Wood, 1981) but few equivalent investigations are available at the level of individual classrooms or specific tests. Thus, although the Neale test has been widely used for over 25 years and has featured in major research studies (e.g. Rutter et al., 1970) there are no documented accounts of how or why it is used or, indeed, who uses it. This raised problems in tailoring the design of the new test to a particular type of user and in deciding which features should be preserved or discarded.

Informal and anecdotal sources suggested that originally the Neale test had been of considerable importance to educational psychologists and that as schools psychological services developed, its use had extended to teachers in associated remedial and support teams. It seemed likely that such users found the test useful for simultaneous diagnostic and normative assessment and that the availability of three Forms was important for evaluating remedial progress. How far this could be the basis for suppositions about its future use is unclear. As Gillham (1978) exemplifies, some educational psychologists are increasingly questioning the role of norm-referenced testing in their work. Similarly, Gipps and Goldstein (1984) draw attention to possible changes in the role and work of LEA remedial teams. These might have implications for future testing practices.

In any case, use by such specialist agencies cannot entirely account for the popularity of the Neale test. It appears to have enjoyed a considerable following in schools. For example, some primary teachers use it as the basis for reading interviews with children or for screening and progress testing across complete year groups. In developing the NMRA we were conscious that the contexts in which it would be used were diverse and that the expertise, resources and purposes of future users would vary greatly.

A question which recurred during the project was that of how far test users observe the prescribed procedures and guidelines for administering and interpreting reading tests. A number of writers have proffered practical guidance on the testing and assessment of reading (e.g. Pumfrey 1977; Vincent, 1985; Dobbins, 1985). Yet how far such prescriptive accounts can be treated as descriptive of actual or orthodox practice remains open to question. There are certainly two major categories of potential 'unorthodoxy' which it seemed important to consider in developing the NMRA.

First, it appears that many users of established individual reading tests have developed their own particular ways of using the test materials which they have found diagnostically valuable. Such creative and extemporary uses were anticipated in the case of the Neale test. The manual advises that during testing the administrator may abandon the procedures for normative scoring in order to pursue diagnostic assessment and that 'in the hands of the experienced teacher or examiner it offers unlimited opportunities for making more subtle assessments' (p.34).

It is possible that a substantial and diverse body of innovative clinical styles of using the Neale test has evolved since its publication in 1958. Sadly, these remain like unrecorded or uncollected folk-songs. Any expertise which has developed in using the original test was unavailable in any systematic form which could have informed the design of the new instrument. Indeed, there is a general dearth of evidence concerning the 'diagnostic facts of life'. The question of what skilled diagnosticians do, and how efficacious it is, seems overdue for investigation. Findings from such studies which have been conducted give no grounds for complacency. Vinsonhaler et al. (1983) found that skilled diagnosticians, working with simulated cases of reading difficulty, displayed little agreement about the nature of the difficulties exhibited by the same case. Agreement over remedial prescriptions for a case was also low and there was little intra-individual consistency in initial and re-diagnosis of the same case.

A second problem is that of unintentional or misinformed departures from correct or recommended administration and scoring procedures. Gipps et al. (1983) encountered such examples of 'human fallibilty' in test use (p. 130) and in early trials of NMRA materials we found ourselves accidentally failing to observe important details in the administration procedures we had devised. Similar errors on the part of project fieldworkers were also detected. Slee (1985) refers to a comparable example of errors made by teachers in giving the Standard Reading Tests (Daniels and Diack, 1958). It is thus worth asking how extensive such 'contamination' in testing has been in the past and what account should be taken of it by developers of future tests.

Tester variations: precision in assessing oral accuracy

The NMRA was standardised by testing some 600 children in the seven- to 12-year-old age range. Testing was carried out by a team of 13 paid fieldworkers. All fieldworkers underwent a half day training in administering the materials. This included practice in scoring audio recordings of test performance and feedback on the appropriateness and accuracy of the scores they had given. A detailed analysis of their later attempts revealed that during a single playback of a test session all fieldworkers tended to underestimate the true number of oral reading errors made, especially on passages where readers made relatively large numbers of errors. In fact, as many as three or four playbacks were needed to note all the errors when preparing the training recordings. There was neither time nor resources to analyse results exhaustively for the standardisation children in this way, nor would many teachers have the time to do this when using the test. However, the NMRA followed the Neale test in requiring testing to be discontinued after 16 errors are made on a passage. This would tend to mitigate the effects of the tendency to underestimate precise numbers of errors made as readers reached their 'ceiling' of difficulty on the test. Nevertheless, this finding suggests that more vigilant users of the test may unwittingly apply the norms more stringently. The question of how accurately oral reading tests in general are customarily scored merits fuller investigation.

Reliability of individual reading tests

Test manuals conventionally express their tests' reliability as a numerical reliability coefficient. It is tempting to treat such indices as intrinsic properties of the tests. Our findings challenge this assumption as far as certain types of individual reading tests are concerned.

Reliability of the NMRA was established by testing each child in the standardisation group on two Forms (A + B; A + C; B + C). Fieldworkers were instructed to arrange to retest on the soonest convenient separate day whenever possible. These arrangements had to meet the requirements of participating schools. Thus actual times between initial and retesting varied from unavoidable same-day retesting to retesting over a week later.

Reliability of oral accuracy testing

Results for oral accuracy were prepared for NMRA by totalling the errors made and subtracting the result from 100 - exact details of the procedure are to be found in the manual. Inter-form correlations for both accuracy and comprehension scores are given in Table 1, together with comparable inter-form correlations for the Neale.

Table 1: Inter-form Correlations (Pearson's r)

	Accuracy		Comprehension	
	r	n	r	n
A with B				
Macmillan	.94	206	.83	174
Neale	.98	100	.97	100
A with C				
Macmillan	.91	191	.79	165
Neale	.98	100	.96	100
B with C				
Macmillan	.91	208	.76	187
Neale	(not reported)			

The Neale results are consistently higher. It is likely that a wider range of ability existed in Neale's sample. This would account partly for the higher figures obtained by Neale. However,

Table 2: Inter-form correlations of oral accuracy
scores for individual fieldworkers

Test Forms

	A + B		A + B		A + C	
Fieldworker:	r	n	r	n	r	n
1	.98	13	–	0	.84	12
2	.97	8	.94	7	.99	7
3	.95	5	.71	7	.98	5
4	.95	15	.97	17	.93	15
5	.95	20	.94	21	.90	25
6	.93	6	.77	6	.74	8
7	.94	49	.92	45	.93	49
8	.92	24	.91	14	.82	26
9	.92	13	.92	13	.94	14
10	.96	9	.90	8	.65	8
11	.94	23	.93	27	.90	22
12	.93	12	.65	8	.92	9
13	.92	8	.83	5	.93	6

differences in in the method of retesting may also be important. Neale (1956) reports that all children were tested on two Forms in a single session. This could have led to more consistent results than in the current study where the minimum break was half a day and the maximum over a week. Also, all testing for the Neale was carried out by the author herself rather than by a team. This may also have helped to ensure a high level of consistency in testing. As Table 2 shows, different fieldworkers can vary in the reliability of their accuracy test-retest scores. Although few were able to match Neale's level most seem capable of obtaining at least one correlation above 0.9 although there are isolated cases of 0.8 and less with one result as low as 0.15.

The results should not be attributed entirely to fieldworker fallibility. Many of the correlation coefficients are based on small numbers and their pattern of distribution is far from systematic. This supports the interpretation that they could be partly an outcome of sampling error. For example, Fieldworker 12 obtained two acceptably reliable results (for Forms A + B and B + C) but one low result (for Forms A + C). It is implausible that the fieldworker 'became' unreliable when giving Forms A and C but 'reverted' to being reliable when giving the two other combinations of Forms. If the three results are treated as separate estimates of this fieldworker's reliability it would be safe to say this individual could generally be expected to obtain reliable results. This might be a less safe assumption in the case of Fieldworkers 3 and 6. Both obtained two unreliable results and these might reflect a genuine inconsistency.

These findings are a useful indication of the likely reliability of future users of the test: while most users can expect to obtain results of adequate reliability this cannot be unreservedly assumed. Some form of self-checking based on

retesting at least ten readers would be
desirable.

The results also give rise to reflections on
the way test reliability is established.
Understandably, test constructers exercise
considerable care and control in trials and
standardisation of a new test. The effect of this
care may be to exclude precisely those extraneous
conditions which will actually attend future use
of a test.

Reliability and validity of comprehension
testing

Comprehension scores on the NMRA are based on the
number of comprehension questions correctly
answered. The general influences discussed in
relation to oral accuracy would again explain

Table 3: Inter-form correlations of comprehension scores for individual fieldworkers

Test Forms

	A + B		A + B		A + C	
	r	n	r	n	r	n
Fieldworker:						
1	.92	13	-	0	.78	12
2	.95	7	.90	7	.96	7
3	.94	5	.69	7	.92	5
4	.81	16	.83	17	.82	15
5	.84	15	.87	13	.78	18
6	.79	6	.98	5	.74	8
7	.88	39	.76	39	.82	44
8	.63	18	.78	13	.57	23
9	.55	11	.60	10	.87	14
10	.20	7	.87	7	.87	6
11	.84	21	.82	24	.76	22
12	.74	12	.97	7	.80	9
13	-	(4)	-	(3)	-	(2)

partly the difference between the two tests. However, Table 1 showed not only that Neale reliability figures are somewhat higher than for NMRA but that on both tests comprehension reliability is lower than for accuracy. The pattern of individual fieldworker reliability in scoring comprehension is shown in Table 3.

It will be seen that a number of fieldworkers failed to obtain any test-retest correlations above 0.9 and inter- and intra-fieldworker variability is generally greater than for accuracy. The less satisfactory performance of the comprehension questions can be explained in terms of the problematic nature of oral comprehension testing.

The mode of testing requires that once a passage has been read aloud a number of questions are presented and answered orally. Time for reflection before answering is limited. The reader is permitted to look back briefly at the text before responding but is not permitted to search the passage word by word for a piece of text which would provide or constitute an answer. The administrator has to decide whether each answer is right or wrong, referring to an answer key in the test manual where necessary.

This procedure appeals to intuitions about informal methods of checking for reading with understanding. However, its development into a formal testing method creates a number of problems. Initial trials of questions revealed that in many cases the difficulty of the task resided in understanding the question rather than the aspects of text to which it was intended to refer. Pollitt and Hutchinson (this volume) present a systematic analysis of determinants of question difficulty which can intervene between reader and text in group pencil and paper tests. Similar effects probably obtain in individual oral testing.

To such textual problems must be added the effect of the social context of testing. The way a question is interpreted will be related to the social context in which it is asked. Fyfe (1979) in a study involving the Neale comprehension questions concludes that social knowledge and experience affect the the strategies children employ in responding to the questions. In particular, a reader must have the capacity to infer correctly that convergent and literal responses would be appropriate rather than inferential responses going beyond the text. Guthrie (1984) and Street (1984) discuss examples of how cultural and social mismatch between mode of questioning, perspective of tester and those tested can produce misleading results. It is arguable that even where cultural differences are minimised such differences of intention, perspective and expectation may exist.

Heap (1980) presents a convenient overall scheme for categorising such difficulties. He identifies three 'organizational assessment problems' which can invalidate reading assessment: resource problems, barrier problems and frame problems. Resource problems arise where a correct answer is based on processes other than those the test is intended to measure. For example, Allington et al. (1977) demonstrated that comprehension test questions often could be correctly answered without reading the passages. Barrier problems occur where a wrong answer is precipitated by features of the test rather than absence of the intended skill. This happens where a reader is deterred from giving a correct answer because the required answer has been given, albeit wrongly, to an earlier question. Frame problems arise where an incorrect answer is attributable to 'a difference in the student's frame of reference for understanding and completing the task'. One of the passages in the NMRA is a recipe for cooking rice. The early trial questions ended with 'What sort of book do you think this comes from?' Some of the very few children who did not answer in the terms expected replied to the effect that it was 'part of a test'. It appears that the expression and intonation the administrator used to signal '... now this is the final question' led them to assume the test session had finished. For them the implicit rules of the testing game no longer applied and the frame of reference within which they answered was changed. Heap's own examples are taken from classroom observation of informal oral tasks and questions posed by the teacher, but they apply also to formal modes of testing, particularly individual oral testing.

Heap's purpose is to demonstrate the limits to the validity of reading tests. His analysis is also relevant to the problem of reliability in the case of the NMRA. The number of comprehension questions attempted by younger or less proficient readers is restricted by the need to discontinue testing once a ceiling of difficulty is reached. This increases the relative impact of 'dubious' questions on results to the detriment of reliability as well as validity in Heap's terms. Field trials of prototypes allowed elimination of systematically problematic questions but the potential for idiosyncratic interactions of reader and question inevitably remained. Heap's account is an effective rehearsal of the potential sources of 'random' error in reading tests.

It is possible that test administrators may be sometimes sensitive to the effect of resource, barrier and frame upon readers' answers because of the quality and manner of answering. This could provide diagnostic opportunities not easily afforded by group tests. It is certainly desirable that awareness of these problems should generally guide the judgement of readers' answers. In any event, the testing format of the NMRA places a premium upon the administrator's ability to make immediate judgements about a complex and subtle phenomenon.

Apart from the exercise of teacher scepticism, Heap's solution to the dilemma he poses is to call for diversity in format of assessment to allow reading competence to show 'through the collective differences in format resources and barriers.' The variety of question types is preserved in the final version of the NMRA and in a small way this meets the diversity criterion. Paradoxically, this variation probably did little to increase reliability.

The greatest difficulty associated with individual oral comprehension tests is the pressure for immediacy in response and in judgement. A silent group test requiring written answers allows contemplation of both question and answer. Heap would argue that a change to this group format simply introduces a different set of resource, barrier and frame problems. Even so, we would argue that silent group comprehension tests allow readers time to select and revise the resources and frame in a way which is likely to match the intended requirements of the test rather than to confound them. Of course, the point of a test such as the NMRA is that it is suitable for appraisal in clinical one-to-one situations. However, the possibility of giving silent individual tasks to be worked at a pace determined by the reader has been largely neglected by test constructors.

Bias in testing

The standardisation data also provided evidence of bias in the relative severity with which fieldworkers assessed readers' performance. Table 4 presents the extent by which the mean score awarded by each fieldworker deviated from the overall pooled mean score awarded by all fieldworkers for accuracy and comprehension i.e. the grand mean for the complete standardisation group.

Table 4: Individual deviations of mean scores
awarded by fieldworkers from overall
mean

	Accuracy			Comprehension		
	A	B	C	A	B	C
Fieldworker:						
1	-5.1	-4.0	-1.9	-0.7	0.2	0.3
2	10.1	6.3	10.7	1.4	1.6	1.7
3	3.4	2.4	-0.6	-1.0	-0.5	-5.6
4	1.5	1.3	0.2	1.3	0.3	0.8
5	1.5	2.6	1.0	0.2	-0.2	-0.3
6	-5.5	-8.4	-12.0	-4.2	4.2	-4.8
7	-1.4	-1.0	-1.5	-0.1	-0.2	-0.9
8	2.8	3.1	1.7	1.7	1.2	1.4
9	-0.3	-2.6	1.4	1.7	1.5	1.7
10	-0.5	5.8	3.0	-2.3	-1.5	-0.6
11	-0.5	-0.9	-1.3	-0.1	0.1	1.2
12	-1.0	-5.5	2.2	-0.7	-1.7	1.5
13	-0.5	0.0	4.3	-1.6	1.7	0.3
F Ratio	3.652	6.726	5.049	7.259	5.810	5.960
P	<.001	<.001	<.001	<.001	<.001	<.001

These average scores were adjusted to take
account of any differences in the actual ages of
the children that the fieldworkers were assigned
to test. The variations between adjusted mean
scores for both accuracy and comprehension were
found to be statistically significant on all
three Forms. Such a finding is perhaps not
surprising and is compatible with the earlier
observation that true oral error rates tend to be
underestimated. The more vigilant tester will be
the more severe.

However, the actual range of the difference
between most of the average scores awarded is
generally modest. Also, it appears that

fieldworkers were generally consistent in scoring leniently or stringently. This could indeed be taken as a re-assuring indication that for the most part future users of the NMRA are unlikely to be seriously capricious or divergent in the rigour with which they assess readers. Nevertheless, the findings support the case for precautions of a sort which have probably been overlooked in the past. Comparison of results obtained by different administrators must be made with caution, if at all. Where possible, calibration exercises should be carried out so that something is known about a tester's relative bias towards leniency or stringency. If serious decisions are to be based on test results serious efforts to take account of administrator bias would be needed. Is it also worth asking whether the findings might reflect in a salutory fashion on past use of tests such as the Neale Analysis of Reading Ability?

Some conclusions - need for training

Gillham (1978) refers to the 'psychology of test-giving behaviour' as a neglected subject in the debate about psychological testing. Johnston and Allington (1983) also point out that individual testing is a social event in which interaction of administrator and test taker will influence the result and interpretation of the test. These are certainly dimensions of testing which need to be better understood. Although the NMRA has many of the psychometric attributes of 'objective' group tests of reading, it would be foolhardy to regard its administration as objective in the sense applied to group tests.

The problem might be responded to through greater attention to the training of future test users. A noteworthy example of how such provision could be developed is the Barking Diagnostic Reading Battery (Trickey and Daly, 1979). In this case the constructors of an individual diagnostic test for use within an LEA have continued to provide training courses in the use of their materials. Teachers who complete a course are certified as recognised users of the test.

It would be less easy to provide such training for the NMRA which is designed for distribution on a national and commercial basis, although the authors propose to explore the possibility for intending users. The scope of this 'centre-to-periphery' strategy is likely to be limited. It would be certainly both desirable and feasible for schools or LEAs to organise their own self-training programmes for intending users of the NMRA. Ideally, these should include the following elements:

1. Review of policy concerning the role and use of testing;

2. Verification that the NMRA is appropriate for purposes identified in 1;

3. Close study and discussion of the NMRA manual;

4. Checks - in the form of oral or written tests - that conceptual and procedural aspects of the test have been understood;

5. Group scoring of video and audio record ings of readers attempting the test;

6. Practice and observation of live test sessions;

7. Comparison of results to check individual reliability and severity/leniency.

Initiation of activities along these lines presupposes a substantial commitment and a concern to ensure that testing is conducted and interpreted correctly. Individual reading tests have been used in British schools for many years without great attention having been paid to such

77

training. The subject has only recently begun to exercise test constructors. Diagnosis and Remediation of Handwriting Problems by Stott et al. (1985) provides an interesting example of a recent initiative in this respect which makes explicit recommendations for scorer training.

It has to be acknowledged that there are circumstances in which the alternative of dispensing with tests altogether - the NMRA included - rather than permitting their unsatisfactory use could be preferable. Less radically, use of group objective tests may serve the purpose of testing just as well as an individual instrument. Nevertheless, there will remain situations in which it is judged - however reluctantly - that an individual test needs to be used to obtain normative scores. If it is so important to have these, it is likely that considerable importance will be attached to them. If professional decisions are to be based upon test results, professional rigour should underlie the means of obtaining them.

References

Allington, R.L., Chodos, L., Domaracki, J. and Truex, S. (1977) Passage dependency: four diagnostic oral reading tests. The Reading Teacher, 30, 369-375.

DES (1975) A Language for Life. (The Bullock Report). London: HMSO.

Durrell D.D. (1955) Durrell Analysis of Reading Difficulty. New York: Harcourt, Brace Jovanovich.

Dobbins, D.A. (1985) How teachers can use the diagnostic-remedial method to improve attainment in reading: and example. Remedial Education, 20 (2) 79-85.

Fyfe, R. (1979) Early difficulties in reading comprehension. Education in the North, 16, 45-50.

Gillham, B. (1978) The failure of psychometrics. In B. Gillham (Ed.) **Reconstructing Educational Psychology.** London: Croom Helm.

Gipps, C. and Wood, R. (1981) The testing of reading in LEAs: The Bullock Report seven years on. **Educational Studies,** 7 (2) 133-143.

Gipps, C. and Goldstein, H. (1984) More than a change in name? **Special Education Forward Trends** 11 (4) 6-8.

Gipps, C., Steadman, S., Blackstone, T. and Stierer, B. (1983) **Testing Children.** London: Heinemann Educational Books.

Guthrie, J.T. (1984) Contexts for testing. **Reading Teacher,** 38 (1) 108-110.

Heap, J.L. (1980) What counts as reading: limits to certainty in assessment. **Curriculum Inquiry,** (10) 3 265-291.

Johnston, P.H. and Allington, R.L. (1983) Commentary: How sharp is a unicorn's horn? **Reading Research Quarterly,** 18 (4) 498-500.

Morris, J.M. (1984) Phonics: from an unsophisticated past to a linguistics-informed future. In G. Brooks and A.K. Pugh (Eds.) Studies in the History of Reading. Reading: Centre for the Teaching of Reading, University of Reading School of Education.

Neale, M.D. (1956) **The Construction and Standardisation of a Diagnostic Reading Test in a Survey of the Reading Attainments and Attitudes of Primary School Children.** Unpublished Ph.D. Thesis, University of Birmingham.

Neale, M.D. (1966) **Neale Analysis of Reading Ability.** (2nd Edn.) London: Macmillan.

Pumfrey P.D. (1977) **Measuring Reading Abilities.** London: Hodder and Stoughton.

Rutter, M., Tizard, J. and Whitmore K. (Eds.) (1970) Education, Health and Behaviour. London: Longmans.

Slee, F. (1985) How useful is the Daniels and Diack Test One? Remedial Education, 20 (2) 64-67.

Stott, D.H., Moyes, F.A. and Henerson, S.E. (1985) Diagnosis and Remediation of Handwriting Problems. Guelph, Ontario: Brook Educational Publishing.

Street B.V. (1984) Literacy in Theory and Practice. (Chapter 1) Cambridge: Cambridge University Press.

Trickey J. and Daly, B. (1979) The Barking Project. In M.St.J. Raggett, C. Tutt C. and P. Raggett (Eds.) Assessment and Testing of Reading. London: Ward Lock Educational.

Vincent, D. (1985) Reading Tests in the Classroom: an introduction. Windsor: NFER-Nelson.

Vincent, D. and de la Mare, M. (1985) The New Macmillan Analysis of Reading Ability. London: Macmillan.

Vinsonhaler, J., Weinshank, A.B., Wagner, C.C. and Polin, R.M. (1983) Diagnosing children with educational problems: Characteristics of reading and learning disabilities specialists, and classroom teachers. Reading Research Quarterly, 3 (18) 134-164.

Cloze Procedure in the Diagnostic Assessment of Silent Reading

Helen Mulholland

The remedial teaching of reading has been one of the growth industries of the last twenty years. Large numbers of children are now recognised as having reading difficulties, that is difficulties in developing reading to a level at which the effective use of text becomes possible. These increasing numbers may result from greater demands in literacy related to general changes in society, or to real or perceived changes in 'standards of literacy' within the education system. The response has been the employment of an increasing number of remedial teachers, whose function is not the teaching of reading but the overcoming of difficulties which have arisen in the course of reading development.

The remedial teacher in a secondary school has available large amounts of published material specifically designed to 'remedy' the situation. Unfortunately, there has been a significant lack of material created for purposes of description of the problem of their older, failing readers, whose failure must be seen in relation to the normal activities in reading undertaken by their chronological peers.

While there is still a significant amount of oral reading in Scottish secondary schools, it is expected that pupils of this age will be able to read silently and to comprehend what they read. Remedial teaching directed towards oral reading is insufficient for their needs and may even be considered inappropriate for their age. It may also be argued that they have already experienced seven years of reading teaching with an oral reading bias and that this has met with little success. The secondary remedial teacher must therefore be concerned with silent reading.

Difficulties in the assessment of silent reading are considerable. Nevertheless, cloze procedure appears to offer a way to monitor readers' reactions at various points during their interaction with a text. The report which follows does not claim that responses obtained on cloze tests may automatically be assumed to 'mirror' normal reading behaviour. The reader, in completing a cloze test, is probably operating on a representation of the text which is specific to the cloze task rather than creating the type of text base for storage in long term memory which would be the product of normal silent reading. The processing requirements of cloze tests will reflect some, but not all, of the features of reading for information.

Cloze responses may provide insights into readers' awareness of the existence of different types of information at different points in a text, and into their ability to synthesise appropriate information. A primary purpose of the author's research was to investigate which aspects of the interaction with text were susceptible to observation by the use of the cloze procedure. If the results of such observation could be supported by evidence from studies using other methods of investigation, their validity would be increased. This paper includes some of this supporting evidence.

The studies

The responses which formed the basis of the system of analysis were obtained from two studies (Mulholland, 1984). In the first, failing readers at age twelve were compared with normal readers at age nine, with whom they were matched in terms of scores on a standardised reading test. They were also compared with normal readers of their own chronological age.

In the second study, the responses of samples drawn from the top, middle and bottom fifteen per cent of a secondary school population in terms of cloze scores, were compared. The materials used were the same throughout - two passages of narrative and two of expository material, each of around 100 words and each having 15 deletions. All of the deletions were nouns or verbs. Various forms and presentations of the material were used; these will be referred to when they relate to the findings of the analysis of responses.

To date, the number of responses analysed is over 200,000. The subjects, over 3,000, range in age from eight to 16 years.

The classification system

Previous systems of analysis of cloze responses have related the responses to the text in terms of syntactic, semantic or morphological appropriateness (Neville and Pugh, 1977), or have related responses to constraints from different ranges within the text (Oller, 1972). Lopardo and Bartnick (1977) outlined a method of using cloze to carry out a reading inventory but the method was applied to individual responses as they occurred and no fixed classification system was included.

The system which is required for diagnostic purposes must relate responses to the behaviour of the reader. It may be argued that any such system will be subjective, reflecting not what the reader did or thought, but what the rater thinks the reader did or thought. It was for this reason that the system did not originate in an attempt to fit a theoretical framework onto the responses but in an 'open' analysis of all the words offered.

It was established at an early stage that all responses could be fitted into four groups: no response, correct response, error related to the theme of the text, and error having no relationship to the theme of the text.

1. Non-responses

The lay-out used was a standard twelve space gap with a broken line to mark the position of each deletion; it is unlikely, but possible, that some responses arose from the overlooking of gaps. In the majority of cases, however, it was assumed that a non-response indicated some degree of difficulty occurring for that reader at that point. Nine-year-olds left more non-responses than older readers of equivalent reading ability. While non-responses tell us nothing about the method of reading, they may indicate attitude; it seems that a more logical approach is being adopted when a blank is left than when the entry is a word which has no connection with any part of the context.

2. Correct responses

Two types of correct responses were counted. Exact-words deleted from the text were recorded as verbatim scores. All other responses offered were listed and submitted to a panel of teachers of English who judged which responses were to be rated 'acceptable'. These were words which correctly restored the original meaning and structure of the text. They were recorded as semantically acceptable scores.

It appeared that the ability to restore the exact word, rather than a synonym, increased slightly between age nine and secondary age groups but was significantly related to ability but not to age in the secondary school. Variation with ability was significant beyond the 0.001 level.

One of the criticisms of the cloze procedure has been in this area and many authorities have devised complex scoring systems to discriminate between various degrees of acceptability in responses (Bormuth, 1965; Coleman and Miller, 1967). Klein-Braley (1981) has developed a modified form of cloze in which subjects are given the first part of the deleted word to eliminate the 'lexical guessing game' element.

The results of the present research would suggest that, at least for native English speakers, such measures are unnecessary since those who gain higher scores are able to access the exact-word deleted more frequently than less fluent readers who may offer a synonym.

Studies using other techniques have established that vocabulary is the best single predictor of a child's ability to comprehend written material (Rosenshine, 1980), but we must ensure that the relationship between reading and vocabulary development is regarded as a cyclical one and not simply cause and effect.

3. Errors related to the theme of the text

'The minimal condition for the connectedness of propositions ... is their connection with the same (or related) topic(s) of conversation' (Van Dijk, 1977, p.52.).

This minimal condition applies equally to the reading of text as to speech. Readers must be aware of the need to preserve 'coherence' in their reconstruction of the meaning of the text. For this reason, the existence of responses, in all groups of readers, which clearly are not related to the topic of the text is a cause for concern.

It may be argued that this factor is to some extent a reflection of the reader's operating on a strategy which is specific to the cloze test situation. Combining elements as they occur by surface signals of cohesion may lead to a coherent approach over text segments but is unlikely to produce the total cohesion of the text which would result from normal processing directed at creating a text base.

In the responses of good readers, however, only three per cent of all responses belong to the category of non-theme related; in the responses of failing readers, the figure is 17 per cent. This very high figure raises the question of whether failing readers can be said to be processing text in any meaningful way or whether they are merely working through a collection of segments, some of which contain sufficient information for correct restoration of deletions.

It seems clear that non-theme related errors will arise at points of difficulty. Readers' behaviour at such points will depend on their capacity to abide by the 'rules of interaction' which require that they recognise the unity of the text. The ratio of non-theme related errors to theme related errors will show the extent of such willingness at points of difficulty.

In the secondary school study, the ratio was 0.17 for good readers, 0.30 for average and 0.56 for poor readers. For nine-year-olds it was 0.45. 'Coherence' would therefore appear to be a major factor in the effective approach to cloze tests.

A similar effect in other reading related activities is shown by Scardamalia and Bereiter (1984). They report that, in thinking aloud about text during reading, sixth-grade readers engaged in element by element interpretation of text details. Tenth-grade readers also referred to this type of activity but, in addition, were more likely to involve interpretation of larger structures in their strategies. It may therefore be that the development of a macro-structure strategy is a late one, and that the type of processing reflected in the present analysis of cloze responses is a valid reflection of normal reading behaviour for younger and less fluent readers.

Within those responses related to the theme of the text, there are six categories of response.

a) Errors of accuracy of perception
In these cases, the reader appears to have overlooked, or wrongly asssumed the presence of, a small item of print, a punctuation mark or a word of up to three letters.

Only six of the 60 items in the test gave rise to this type of response but it occurred more frequently in the responses of poor and failing readers than of the other groups, including the nine-year-olds. Accuracy of perception appears to play a part in the effective development of reading and has been the subject of many studies.

Killey and Willows (1980) found that poor readers in fourth grade were not able to pinpoint errors in orally presented material and concluded that differences in linguistic sensitivity are relatively stable and long lasting character-istics of individuals. It may be argued that, in reading, lack of practice in sustained silent reading may contribute to this effect but the presence of the effect in the listening condition would appear to support the view that accuracy of perception of language, in whatever mode, may be an area of difficulty for some pupils. In this context, it may be noted that Weaver (1967), on the basis of eye-movement research, reported that 75 per cent of two letter words were 'skipped', that is, not fixated, in silent reading. Such 'un-attended' print has been shown by Willows (1974) to be a source of information for good but not for poor readers. The incidence of more errors of accuracy in the reading of poor readers may arise from a combination of these two effects. The failing reader may have progressed to a stage at which fixations are not located on 'small' words and the presence of such a word outside the area of focus of the fixation may provide less information than it does to the good reader.

b) Errors of structure
These occur when the reader has failed to restore the syntax of the original text. They occurred on only three of the 60 items and were more frequent in the responses of both younger and failing readers.

Since the syntax of the texts used was fairly simple, giving a predicted readability level of nine to ten years, it seems likely that normal readers developed the ability to handle the few structural difficulties between the ages of nine and 12. The failure of the less able readers to do so may relate to their different experience of printed language structures.

Bormuth (1966) found that poor readers' comprehension of printed material was improved when the sentence structure resembled that of spoken language. Smiley et al. (1978) report that poor readers' comprehension of a story was not improved by having the story read to them. These results would indicate that it is a lack of familiarity with the specific structures used in printed language, rather than with reading as a specific mode of language use, which may be creating difficulty for the less fluent reader.

c) Errors of vocabulary
In these responses, the reader has correctly restored the structure of the original text but has failed to provide a word which is sufficiently close in meaning to the original to be deemed acceptable. This type of response is made by all groups of readers with equal frequency.

d) Errors of expectation
Here the reader creates a text which is correct both in structure and in meaning but differs from the original. Since this type of response shows

readers actively adding to the text from their own store of knowledge, it is an indication of good reading behaviour in the absence of visual cues. It is proportionately more frequent in the responses of good readers than of other groups.

In the first study carried out by the author, one form of test consisted of presenting the material as a series of isolated sentences. Under these conditions, the groups of normal 12-year-old readers generated a greater number of different responses than either the nine-year-olds or the failing readers. When the whole continuous text was present, the number of different responses was the same for all three groups.

Theories regarding anticipation in reading have postulated that it takes place at varying levels of consciousness from the fully formed surface structure 'prediction' (Weaver, 1980), to hypothesis generation (Woods, 1980), and the activation of appropriate schemes and scenarios (Sanford and Garrod, 1981). Since the evidence from the previous study suggests that the good reader at age 12 is able to see more possible interpretations within a sentence, it would appear that this facility in anticipation is an important aspect of reading development which is occurring between age nine and age 12.

e) Errors of hesitation
Some responses appear to have arisen from the readers failing to make use of context following the deletion. This occurs in both theme related and non-theme related responses and confirms the findings of Neville and Pugh (1977) in that less fluent readers produce more responses of this type.

It seemed possible that the physical presence of a gap in the text might be contributing to this effect but a study in which no gap was left to mark the site of the deletion indicated that this was not the case.

Potter (1981) found that all readers tended to look ahead before recording a response on cloze tests and it may be that the use of information from following context is related, not to looking at text, but to the ability to pick up information and/or to relate it to the restoration of the deletion. Failing readers may see the visual symbols but fail to attend to the information they contain, or they may attend to the information but fail to perform the logical processing necessary to relate it to the preceding information.

Since individual deletions varied in their predictability, i.e. the extent to which they could be restored on the basis of preceding context, the presence of errors of hesitation is not constant but varies considerably between items.

f) Random errors
Readers who were following the theme of the text but experiencing difficulty with local context occasionally inserted words which, though related to the theme, had no connection with local structure or meaning. This occurred more often in the responses of younger and less fluent readers but accounted for less than two per cent of all responses.

4. Errors which are not related to the theme of the text

a) Errors which are correct within the sentence
These arise when the reader recognises the need to treat the sentence as a unit, but fails to connect the sentence to other parts of the text. Eight per cent of the responses of average readers in secondary school came into this category as did ten per cent of the responses of nine-year-olds. The development of the ability to make connections between sentences is therefore an important area for consideration in the teaching of 'normal' readers. A more recent study, not yet fully analysed, indicated that by age eight, good readers produce only two per cent of responses of

this type and only 13 per cent which do not relate to the theme of the text.

One aspect of text structure which was related to significant variation in the pattern of response was the difference between noun and verb deletion. It appeared that verbs were generally more difficult than nouns to restore but that responses to verb deletions were more likely to be related to the theme of the text. When the theme was ignored, however, responses to nouns were more likely to reflect the use of the whole sentence unit than responses to verbs.

This raises another major question with regard to the cloze procedure. It appears that, even when two deletions give rise to the same frequency of correct response, it cannot be assumed that they are truly 'equivalent' unless they produce the same pattern of errors. This aspect of the classification system may prove of value in the investigation of effects of text structure.

b) Errors which relate only to the preceding part of the sentence
These errors decrease in occurrence with both age and ability. Treating the sentence as a unit was shown to be a major distinguishing factor between normal readers at age 12 and both younger and less fluent readers. More than half of the 12-year-olds could restore 23 of the 60 items on the basis of within-sentence information alone; for the other two groups the corresponding figure was nine out of 60 items.

A special problem of the cloze procedure is the violation, by deletion, of phrase and sentence structure. It appears that this violation may have a less important effect on good readers who have been shown to be aware of phrase boundaries before they have 'reached' them in normal reading (Levin and Kaplan, 1970). The deletion site may appear to them in its correct position in the phrase structure; less fluent readers may attempt to use the deletion site as a phrase boundary and thus experience greater syntactic violation.

A study by the author has indicated that this effect persists even when the deletion site is not marked by a physical gap in the text (Mulholland, 1984). This study was designed to assess to what extent a physical gap in the text was contributing to the lack of use of following contexts. Readers were asked to locate the positions in the text from which deletions had been made by inserting a vertical line between any two words which, in their opinion, were adjacent to a deletion. They were then asked to write the missing word at the top of the line. For all readers, this task proved more difficult on deletions of verbs than of nouns but good readers were significantly better than poor readers at locating deletion sites.

Difficulties of recognition of phrase structure may play a significant part in the performance of failing readers on cloze tests. Depending on the position of the deletion, the preceding words may or may not cross a phrase boundary making the structure more or less difficult to re-create.

Cromer (1970) found that the comprehension of poor readers could be improved by marking phrase boundaries. Cloze responses reflect in this respect a difference which has been found in other types of investigation. Perfetti and Lesgold (1977) concluded that difficulties of word recognition and local structure played a greater role in reading failure than difficulties at higher levels of processing. Evidence from the present research would indicate that, when the reader is following the theme of the text, these difficulties are localised and do not produce a great degree of difficulty. Responses which do not relate to the theme of the text show this influence to a much greater degree. A critical area for future investigation is to assess to what extent syntactic difficulties are a cause, and to what extent a result, of the reader's inability to follow the theme of the text.

c) Errors which relate to purely local context
These responses of collocation occur equally in the responses of all groups and account for only three per cent of all responses.

d) Nonsense responses
These are words which bear no apparent relation to any part of the text. Their occurrence decreases with age and with reading ability.

This classification system, when applied to the responses of the six groups of readers, indicated significant differences between groups and within groups between different types of deletion. Differences which were significant may all be supported by evidence from other types of investigation. It appears that the system has some validity.

Within the group of poor and failing readers, it was also possible to see tendencies for individuals to make certain types of error. It seemed that a 'normal' pattern of response could be discerned and that the responses of individuals could be compared with this pattern for diagnostic purposes.

Application of system to diagnostic assessment

By looking at the comparative frequency of occurrence of responses of each type, it is possible to see whether an individual may have problems of:

accuracy of perception
handling syntax
vocabulary
active involvement with text
'reading ahead' for relevant information
making connections between sentences
treating the text as a logical whole.

Remedial activities can then be directed to the necessary aspects of reading. Activities such as cloze procedure, proof reading, group prediction, sequencing and text analysis, all serving as the basis of group discussion, have proved useful in this respect. By using remedial teaching time for these activities, with no oral reading, word recognition or decoding exercises, considerable progress has been made. In one six month programme involving 30 pupils, each pupil spent one 40 minute period per week on these activities. The reading ages of the subjects increased by an average of 24 months and their response patterns on cloze tests became similar to those of normal readers of the same age. Previous remedial programmes had produced increases in reading age of a similar order over a full school year but had not brought about changes in response patterns. These earlier programmes had consisted of word recognition and phonic and reading laboratory activities with less frequent use of structured problem solving discussion.

Brown et al. (1984) report that a programme of discussion activities based on summarising and question setting with readers from the bottom 15 per cent of seventh grade in terms of comprehension, but who had no significant decoding problems, raised their comprehension level to average within 15 days. Since the failing readers in the present study did have decoding problems, it would appear to suggest that Brown et al.'s methods, like those listed above, may have wider usefulness. It may be that the decoding difficulties which are so often used as the basis for diagnostic assessment are related to comprehension difficulties in a more complex way than simple cause and effect and that activities aimed at improving comprehension by discussion will produce rapid improvements in both areas. Use of diagnostic assessment by cloze responses will enable the activities to focus on relevant aspects of text processing.

In The Name of the Rose, Umberto Eco (1984) comments 'When we consider a book, we must ask ourselves not what it says but what it means ...' The classification of responses described in this paper suggests that those who have failed to learn to read effectively may have been concentrating, quite literally, on what the text says and may not have been provided with adequate practice in reading what the text means.

References

Bormuth, J.R. (1965) Validities of grammatical and semantic classifications of cloze test scores. Proceedings of the International Reading Association Conference, Vol. 10, 283-286.

Bormuth, J.R. (1966) Readability: a new approach. Reading Research Quarterly, 1, 79-132.

Brown, A.L., Palincsar, A.S. and Armbruster, B.B. (1984) Instructing comprehension: fostering activities in interactive learning situations. In H. Mandl, N.L. Stein, and T. Trabasso (Eds.) Learning and Comprehension of Text. Hillsdale, N.J.: Erlbaum.

Coleman, E.B. and Miller, G.R. (1967) A set of thirty-six prose passages calibrated for complexity. Journal of Verbal Learning and Verbal Behavior, 6 (6), 851-854.

Cromer, W. (1970) The difference model: a new explanation for some reading difficulties. Journal of Educational Psychology, 61, 471-483.

Eco, Umberto (1984) The Name of the Rose. London: Secker and Warburg.

Killey, J.C. and Willows, D.M. (1980) Good-poor reader differences in detecting, pin-pointing and correcting errors in orally presented sentences. Paper presented at the 1980 Annual

Meeting of the American Educational Research Association, Boston, Mass.

Klein-Braley, C. (1981) The C-test: a modification of the cloze procedure. Paper presented at the 4th International Symposium of the IUS, Colchester.

Levin, H. and Kaplan, E.L. (1970) Grammatical structure and reading. In H. Levin and J.P. Williams (Eds.) Basic Studies in Reading. New York: Basic Books, 119-133.

Lopardo, G.S. and Bartnick, R.M. (1977) A silent inventory based on the cloze procedure. Illinois Schools Journal, 57 (3) 19-23.

Mulholland, H. (1984) The Interaction with Text of Failing and Normal Readers. Unpublished Ph.D. thesis, The Open University.

Neville, M.H. and Pugh, A.K. (1977) Content in reading and listening: variations in approach to cloze tasks. Reading Research Quarterly, 12 (1) 13-31.

Oller, J. (1972) Scoring methods and difficulty levels for cloze tests of proficiency in English as a second language. The Modern Language Journal, 56 (3), 151-158.

Perfetti, C.A. and Lesgold, A.M. (1977) Discourse comprehension and sources of individual differences. Report No. LRDC 1977/1, Pittsburgh University Learning Research and Development Centre.

Potter, F. (1981) The use made of the succeeding linguistic context by good and poor readers. In L.J. Chapman (Ed.) The Reader and the Text. London: Heinemann.

Rosenshine, B.V. (1980) Skill hierarchies in reading comprehension. In R.J. Spiro, B.C. Bruce and W.F. Brewer (Eds.) Theoretical Issues in Reading Comprehension. Hillsdale: N.J.: Erlbaum.

Sanford, A.J. and Garrod, S.C. (1981) Understanding Written Language. Chichester: Wiley.

Scardamalia, M. and Bereiter, C. (1984) Development of strategies in text processing. In H. Mandl, N.L. Stein and T. Trabassso (Eds.) Learning and Comprehension of Text. Hillsdale, N.J.: Erlbaum.

Smiley, S.S., Oakley, D.D., Worthen, D., Campione, J.C. and Brown, A.L. (1978) Recall of thematically relevant material by adolescent good and poor readers as a function of written versus oral presentation. Journal of Educational Psychology, 69, 381-387.

Van Dijk, T.A. (1977) Text and Context. London: Longman.

Weaver, C. (1980) Psycholinguists and Reading: from Process to Practice. Cambridge, Mass: Winthrop.

Weaver, W.W. (1967) The retrieval of learning sets by the external display of reading materials. In G.B. Schick and M. May (Eds.) Junior College and Adult Reading Programs: expanded fields. 16th Yearbook of the Annual Reading Conference. Reprinted in A.J. Kingston (Ed.) Selected Writings of Wendell W. Weaver. Atlanta GA: University of Georgia Press, 1977.

Willows, D.M. (1974) Reading between the lines: selective attention in good and poor readers. Child Development, 45, 408-415.

Woods, W.A. (1980) Multiple theory formation in speech and reading. In R.J. Spiro, B.C. Bruce and W.F. Brewer (Eds.) Theoretical Issues in Reading Comprehension. Hillsdale, N.J.: Erlbaum.

Teacher-Devised Tests: Improving their Validity and Reliability

Frank Potter

Many secondary schools have 'end of year' exams, often to provide a basis for placing children in ability groups, be they 'sets', 'bands' or merely mixed-ability classes. These exams are also often used to show parents how their children perform in relation to their peers.

Until now there have been two ways of doing this - standardised tests, and internal examinations (that is, informal teacher-devised tests). Internal examinations are of unknown reliability, and sometimes lack credibility with outsiders such as parents. On the other hand, standardised tests do not necessarily test what the children have been taught, apart from being costly.

In any case, standardised tests yield more information than is required for the above purposes. All that is really needed is a valid, reliable measure, not a standardised score. One can regard a standardised test as a teacher-devised test that has been through two further psychometric procedures. First, an item analysis has been performed, leading to the selection of the best items in terms of their reliability and facility. We can regard this procedure as resulting in a formal test. The next step in the production of a standardised test is to administer it to a representative sample of the testee population - this provides the information necessary to convert the raw scores into standardised scores. This second step turns the formal test into a standardised test. For the purposes that the end of year examinations serve, all that is really necessary is a formal test. Lunzer, Waite and Dolan's (1979) 'Grieg' test (p.46) is an example of such a formal test.

Constructing a standardised test:

Procedure	Result
Produce items e.g. comprehension questions	Teacher-devised test
Perform item analysis and select the best items	Formal test
Administer to representative sample of testee population to obtain norms	Standardised test

It might be helpful to consider an alternative way of looking at the process of test construction. If a school were to use a standardised test for the above purpose, the raw scores would be enough: there would be no need to convert these scores into standardised scores.

Therefore if a school could 'formalise' its own informal, teacher-devised tests, it could obtain the information it needed more satisfactorily and cheaply. The tests could be devised to cover the skills and strategies that were taught during the year (ensuring content validity), and the formalisation procedure would ensure reliability. Until the advent of the microcomputer this would have been unrealistic, but the item analysis procedure is easily handled by any of the micro-computers now used in schools.

It was with this in mind that the author and two teacher colleagues decided to collaborate on this joint venture. The ultimate goals are (i) to produce a set of valid, reliable, teacher-devised tests (to cover the 11 to 16 age range), (ii) the

99

production of a DIY package which any school could use to produce its own formal tests - without the need for outside specialist help.

We decided to start by performing an item-analysis on the existing first-year English examination, in the school where the author's two collaborators worked, in order to improve its reliability. The reasons for this choice of starting point were that the tests were there and were currently being used, there did not need to be any extra work from the rest of the staff, they did not have to come to any agreement about the content of the tests, nor did we have to try to convince them of any need for change.

In fact, we proceeded with this course of action even though we felt that new tests would eventually have to be devised. The existing tests were short passages with comprehension questions, devised intuitively with no explicit rationale. However, we hoped that having demonstrated the value and feasibility of this approach, we could then include a broader range of items.

There have been three stages in the project so far, a fuller description of which can be found in the appendix.

The existing first-year exams were marked and psychometrically analysed. Some questions were rejected, some revised, and another passage added.

The exam was then given to another group of children, and some more questions rejected. Some rather striking differences were found in the proportion of correct answers to a few of the questions, the worst being a change from 55 per cent correct to six per cent. We thought this might have been because the marking scheme was too loose, so in the third stage it was decided that the scripts would be randomly assigned to three markers.

After the third stage the test had a reliability coefficient of 0.83, close to some published tests of comprehension. The data also confirmed that the markers did indeed differ significantly in their leniency, over 11 of the questions in particular (see appendix for details).

In spite of the final version of the test being fairly reliable, nine of the 31 questions were found to be unreliable (alpha-beater negative: for an explanation of 'alpha-beater' see the appendix). We think that one likely reason is a mismatch between the wording of the questions and the answers expected. To illustrate this point, two of the unreliable questions from the second passage will be discussed.

The Sleeping Warriors
In an enormous cavern somewhere in Scotland lie hundreds of sleeping warriors. They have slumbered for centuries. Their horses are asleep too. They await the breaking of a spell placed upon them hundreds of years ago. They sleep until the time comes when Scotland shall need them.

Outside the cavern hangs a horn upon which three blasts must be blown to rouse the sleepers to action. Once only has the horn been sounded, when a great crisis arose, and the men were needed. Someone went to rouse them. He blew the first blast. The warriors awoke and raised themselves upon their elbows. The horses shook their harness, and champed their bits. This so terrified the messenger that he fled.

There they lie in the darkness of the cavern, awaiting the second and the third blasts that will never come. The horn is still there, too. But alas! no one knows where the cavern is.

Questions

1. Why are the men and horses asleep in the cavern?
2. When, according to the story, will they awaken?
3. How many times must the horn now be blown?
4. What is another word for 'hundreds of years'?
5. When the horn blew, what happened (a) to the men and (b) to the horses?
6. Why has no one gone to rouse the sleepers since that time?

The answer expected for the second question was: 'Never/not at all'. This question was answered correctly by only five per cent of the children, and not only is the alpha-beater index negative, but so is the point-biserial correlation coefficient (the only such instance of a negative point-biserial in the data). Moreover, the analysis in stage 2 led to the same result, and the item was only retained because the teachers concerned were convinced that it should have been a good question - indeed, that this was one of the main points of the passage.

One possible problem here is the misleading nature of the question. The answer expected is that the warriors will never awaken, and yet there is a clear and definitive implication that they will. (When, <u>according to the</u> <u>story</u>, will they awaken?). In addition, there is also a suggestion that the warriors are still awake: they were woken up by the first blast, but it does not state that they went back to sleep - although this may be inferred from the first sentence of the passage.

Given that the teachers concerned are convinced that it should be a good item, we feel that it is worth trying just once more, this time rephrasing the question to something like 'Will they ever awaken?' (and removing 'awoke and' in the second paragraph). This biases the question the other way, but makes it a leading question, rather than a misleading one. In view of the facility level of the item, this might very well be a good thing.

Question 5 was in two parts (two items), namely: 'When the horn blew, what happened (a) to the men? (b) to the horses?' The second part was very reliable, although slightly on the easy side. The first part was, however, not very reliable (point-biserial 0.22; alpha-beater negative). The reason for this seemed to be the result of the marking scheme: credit was given only if the answer contained the information that they awoke and that they raised themselves on their elbows. Twenty-seven per cent of the children volunteered only one of the two parts, and hence were given no credit at all. On the other hand, children did tend to provide both parts of the answer to the second part of the question, almost certainly because they seem to 'go together', to form a 'gestalt' (shook their harness and champed their bits). In fact, it would not have been surprising if children had come unstuck with both parts of this question - strictly speaking nothing happened to the horses, and all that happened to the men was that they were woken up by the blast of the horn. It is slightly strange to describe an active movement as a happening. Most children seemed to have correctly interpreted what the questioners meant to say, rather than what they actually said. But in doing so, it would have been quite intelligent to have made the inference that, as the questioners were obviously after what the horses did, they were also after what the men did - and all they did was to raise themselves on their elbows. If some children did reason in this way, it is not suggested they did so consciously.

The problem with comprehension questions
As we have seen, one of the problems with the test

was to do with the wording of the questions. But this problem is not just that the wording happened to be poor when it could have been good - rather, it reflects the difficulty, or near impossibility, of phrasing questions which are neither leading nor misleading. To put it another way, it seems almost impossible to phrase a question in a way that is specific enough to elicit the desired information, without it also cueing the reader. And this 'cueing' seems to us not simply to make the task easier, but to change its very nature.

It is by no means an original observation that comprehension tests simply reflect children's ability to answer comprehension questions, and not their ability to comprehend. Whilst we have agreed with this observation in the past, it is only now that we realise just how fundamental a problem this is. It is therefore worth spending a little time explaining how we perceive the problem, and how we are trying to solve it.

Recent research (which we shall discuss below), together with our observations, has led us to believe that children probably do indeed adopt different strategies when answering comprehension questions than when attempting to comprehend a passage. The basic difference is whether or not the reader attempts to select the features which are relevant to the understanding of the main idea of the text (making the assumption that the reader's purpose is to try and discover the main idea, which in turn makes the assumption that there is one.)

A point made recently by Evans (1984) can help explain this. He draws a distinction between two types of thought processes, which he terms heuristic and analytic, and describes them thus:

The function of the heuristic process is selection. The outcome of heuristic processing is a judgement of relevance about features of the problem. Information deemed 'irrelevant' is not processed further. 'Relevant' information is then subjected to analytic processing ... the function of analytic processes is to generate some form of inference or judgement from the information selected. (p.451)

Analogously, we think it helpful to think of comprehension as a two stage process: in the first stage the relevant information is selected, and in the second this information is processed to yield some sort of understanding (or misunderstanding). Now it seems to us that these heuristic (or selection) processes are bypassed with most comprehension questions. The information that the reader needs in order to understand the question is precisely the information that renders these heuristic processes unnecessary. In other words the relevant information is selected by the question, rather than by the reader. For example, consider one of Davis' (1968) questions, designed to test 'making inferences about the content':

The delight Tad had felt during his long hours in the glen faded as he drew near the cabin. The sun was nearly gone and Tad's father was at the woodpile. He was wearing the broadcloth suit that he wore to church and to town sometimes. Tad saw his father's hands close around a bundle of wood. He was doing Tad's work - and in his good clothes. Tad ran to him. 'I'll git it, Pa.'

When Tad saw his father, he felt
A   disappointed
B   impatient
C   angry
D   guilty.

Now it seems that this question is little more than a vocabulary item. The testee (reader) is

105

told what information is relevant by the way the question is worded (and even more so by there being a multiple choice), and also by being presented with a short, isolated passage. All the reader has to do is to find which word best matches the behaviour described. (In fact, one could argue that this is exactly the sort of item that one should use to test for knowledge of meaning of words, as to know what 'guilty' means includes knowing what sort of behaviours one would expect from someone who felt this way.)

A question which truly tested the ability to make inferences would have to avoid cueing the reader, so that the readers would select the relevant information for themselves - so that they would have to use heuristic as well as analytic processes. But then the question asked would have to be so general or vague that the reader would not know how to respond.

We will explain how we are attempting to solve this problem later, but first let us examine the implications for the strategies the reader might choose when answering comprehension questions.

If the question selects the relevant features, then on the face of it a reasonable strategy to adopt is the following; look at the question first, check to see if one already knows the answer without having to read the text, and then skim and scan looking for words/phrases etc. relevant to this question.

This strategy would account for Marr and Gormley's (1982) findings, that readers' retellings tended to reflect the information in the passage, whereas their answers to comprehension questions tended to reflect what they already knew (before reading the passage).

In addition, Thomas and Augstein (1972) found that readers performed better on a multiple-choice test when they expected a summary than when they were led to expect multiple-choice questions. This not only supports the hypothesis that readers adopt different strategies in both cases, but also suggests that readers' question-answering strategies are not effective strategies, even for answering comprehension questions.

This may be another reason why the question 'When, according to the story, will they awaken?' was so poorly answered in our test (see above). Adopting the question-answering strategy, the children look for phrases etc. which would answer the question, and in the first paragraph they find 'They sleep until the time comes when Scotland shall need them', and then immediately answer the question. However, later in the passage comes the information which indicates that they 'await the second and third blasts that will never come' as 'no one knows where the cavern is'. If this account is correct, then it would illustrate why children's question-answering strategies are not effective strategies for answering comprehension questions.

Possible solutions

As we are interested in measuring children's comprehension strategies, rather then their question-answering strategies, we are exploring ways in which we can discourage children from using these inefficient question-answering strategies.

One such way is to use a procedure such as Thomas and Augstein's, and lead children to expect a summary (and also make them write a summary), before asking the questions. This may result in a better test of children's comprehension strategies, but it still does not solve the problem of cueing.

Therefore, the other way we are exploring is to try to train children to understand a nonspecific question, such as 'What was the author trying to communicate?' Now, of course texts differ, in that, for example, some have main ideas and some do not, so this task may be quite difficult.

Conclusion

Our main conclusion is that care over the framing of questions, and the production of the marking criteria, is at least as important as subjecting the test to statistical item-selection procedures. On the basis of our work so far, we would recommend adopting the following procedures.

1. Construct the initial test with about twice as many questions as desired in the final test.

2. Make sure that there are a fair number of passages, (about six) each with about the same number of questions (about ten). These questions should be carefully chosen. A variety of passages is important, so that performance on the test is not overly influenced by knowledge of one particular topic.

3. The questions and marking scheme should be given careful consideration by a group of teachers. In particular, the wording of the questions should be examined in conjunction with the answers expected.

4. When the original version of the test has been administered to a large number of children (certainly over 100) in two sittings (as it is twice as long as the final test will be), examples of 'borderline' answers should be listed for each question. Borderline answers are those answers which some markers might be tempted to mark as correct when they are deemed by the setters to be incorrect, and vice versa. This procedure only needs to be done once, and the little bit of extra effort required will be a good investment.

5. The test should be subjected to statistical

analysis, and the best items chosen. Using the microcomputer program we have developed, this is a simple task, and is actually no more time-consuming - the extra time spent entering the information in the computer is balanced by the fact that the computer calculates the children's scores.

However, this procedure makes the assumption that comprehension questions will continue to be used. As we hope we have made clear, we are searching for better means of assessing children's comprehension strategies. Until we have found them, we are forced to continue in this manner, but at least we feel we can improve the existing tests.

Acknowledgement

This was a collaborative venture between the author, Pam Owen and Paul West.

References

Davis, F.B. (1968) Research in comprehension in reading. Reading Research Quarterly, 3, 499-545.

Evans, J. St. B.T. (1984) Heuristic and analytic processes in reasoning. British Journal of Psychology, 75, 451-468.

Lunzer, E., Waite, M. and Dolan, T. (1979) Comprehension and comprehension tests. In E. Lunzer, and K. Gardner (Eds.) The Effective Use of Reading. London: Heinemann Educational.

Marr, M.B. and Gormley, K. (1982) Children's recall of familiar and unfamiliar tests. Reading Research Quarterly, 18, 89-104.

Nunnally, J.C. (1978) Psychometric Theory (2nd edition). New York: McGraw-Hill.

Thomas, L. and Augstein, S. (1972) An experimental approach to the study of reading as a learning skill. Research in Education, 8, 28-46.

Youngman, M.B. (1979) A comparison of item-total point biserial correlation, Rasch and alpha-beater item analysis procedures. Educational Studies, 5, 265-273.

Appendix

There have been three stages in the project so far.

Stage 1 (Summer 1983)

The first year exams were administered as usual. The 125 scripts were marked and the information handed to the author who performed the item analysis. Item-sum correlation coefficients and facility levels were calculated (point-biserial - Nunnally, 1978, p.133). A summary of the results can be found at the end of this appendix. The results of the analysis were then passed back to the collaborating teachers with the following advice:

Item-sum correlation coefficients over 0.30 are satisfactory, those under 0.20 unsatisfactory, while there is scope for improvement for items with coefficients between 0.20 and 0.30 (for example, by changing the wording of the questions). There should be very few items with extreme facility levels (less than 0.20 or more than 0.80), and the average facility level of the test should be around 0.50.

The questions for the first of the three passages were either too easy or unreliable or both (4/5 had facility levels above 0.84). Whilst it may be desirable to retain the passage and questions so that less able children are not overfaced, it is unlikely that the passage itself is worth keeping as part of the scorable test - but it could always be kept and the answers not scored.

There should be at least one other passage added to compensate for the unreliable items.

Stage 2 (Autumn/Spring 1983)

The school revised the first passage completely and also included a totally new passage, as well as modifying or removing other questions. So that a final test would be ready by the end of the year, this new version of the exam was administered to 107 children from another school who were in the first term of their second year.

The results of this analysis revealed that the first passage was no better than before.

In the process of analysing the data, we noticed one or two rather striking discrepancies in the facility level of some items between the two stages. The worst was a change from 0.55 to 0.06. After discussion we concluded that this might be due to the fact that the scripts from stage 2 had been marked by a teacher from the other school, and that the marking schedule had not been tight enough. We also noticed an inexplicable change in the marking scheme for one of the questions on the last passage, which is presumably why it became 'easier' (facility levels changed from 0.23 to 0.49).

As changes in the scoring criteria cast doubt upon the validity of the results of the item analysis, we built into the third stage a procedure to check on the extent of marker agreement.

Stage 3 (Summer 1984)

The easy first passage was discarded, and the most reliable items chosen from the three other passages.

This time the computer was programmed to calculate the alpha-beater index (cf. Youngman, 1979). This is a less arbitrary, and intuitively more acceptable, criterion than the point-biserial correlation coefficient and involves calculating the reliability of the total test with and without the item in question. If the reliability of the total test is worse with the item included then the alpha-beater index is negative. Such items are clearly undesirable. (The term alpha-beater refers to the fact that the reliability of a test is usually calculated using Cronbach's alpha, or a variation of this.)

The scripts were randomly assigned to three markers, and the resulting data statistically analysed, using a one-way analysis of variance, to determine whether there was any significant difference between the marks awarded by the three markers. The result of this analysis is presented in Table 1.

Table 1: Means and standard deviations of the scores awarded by the three markers

	Marker 1	Marker 2	Marker 3
Mean	14.7	16.2	12.8
s.d.	5.0	5.5	5.3
N	63	61	62

There was a statistically significant difference in the marks awarded by the three markers: $F(2,61)=6.46$, $p < 0.01$.

When analysed item by item (using chi squared), there was found to be a statistically significant difference ($p < 0.05$) over the scoring of 11 of the questions.

This version of the test had a reliability coefficient of 0.83 (KR 20), which is close to some published comprehension tests (the GAP Reading Comprehension Test has a reliability coefficient of 0.86). In spite of this, nine of the items were deemed to be unreliable by the (iterative) use of the alpha-beater criterion. The first scan rejected items 1, 5, 8 and 18, the second item 9, the third items 3 and 11, and the fourth items 10 and 16. (Interestingly, for only two of these unreliable items was there significant marker disagreement - namely items 10 and 16.) However, the straightforward elimination of these items was felt to be unwise, for the following three reasons:

1. Because of sampling error (especially as the number of subjects was less than five times the number of items - cf. Nunnally, 1978, p.279). For example, item 5 was found to be reliable in the previous stages (point-biserial coefficients of 0.30 and 0.32) even though the point-biserial coefficient was only 0.12 this time.

2. Because eliminating the nine items would leave the test with only three items covering the first passage, only three items covering the second passage, but with 16 covering the third. Thus, the test would be reduced to little more than a test of comprehension on one of the passages. As performance on a test is bound to be partially a function of passage-specific knowledge, it is always better to sample from a number of texts, rather than just one.

3. Because a qualitative analysis of the items led us to believe that the unreliability of most of these nine items was caused by a mismatch between the wording of the questions and the answers expected, a point discussed in the main text.

Technical data

	stages		
	1	2	3
N of passages	3	4	3
N of items	33	40	31
Mean rpb (point-biserial)	0.27	0.23	0.32
Mean facility level	0.52	0.55	0.47
Reliability (KR20)	0.78	0.76	0.83
No. of items with			
rpb > 0.30	14	14	19
rpb 0.20 - 0.30	9	10	7
rpb < 0.20	10	16	5
alpha-beater negative (iteratively)	N/A	12	9
No. of questions on passage 1	5	5	N/A
No. of questions on passage 2	9	8	6
No. of questions on passage 3	N/A	9	7
No. of questions on passage 4	19	18	18

In stage 2 some of the best items from stage 1 were left out, and some 'surprisingly poor' items included - as a double check. ('Surprisingly poor' items were those which the teachers thought should have been good.)

Just because the number of questions remains similar for a passage does not mean that there were no changes. Some of the questions were modified between stages.

Measuring Attitudes Towards Reading

Peter Pumfrey

The four aims of this paper are:

1. to present an overview of work in this field;

2. to provide sources of information for readers wishing to pursue particular lines of enquiry;

3. to describe some recently developed instruments;

4. to point to some avenues meriting further work.

As travellers, in describing where we are geographically, where we are going and how far we have moved, latitudinal, longitudinal and altitudinal information is of value. Accepting the weaknesses in argument by analogy, it can be shown that cognitive, affective and conative aspects of reading are important in developing an understanding of the reading process. Helping students become competent readers who find the activity a rewarding one is a frequently stated double-barrelled educational objective. An appreciation of changes in both attainments in reading and attitudes towards reading enables us to know whether the educational endeavour is on course. It also directs our attention to the means of best achieving the intended educational ends.

Far more effort has been put into the measurement of cognitive aspects of the reading process than has been spent on the measurement of attitudes towards reading. Whilst in many situations, attainments in, and attitudes towards, reading are positively correlated for groups of learners, there are examples where the relationship is very low. For example, positive attitudes towards reading and low reading attainments are frequently and understandably found in non-English speaking immigrant pupils from developing countries. On the other hand, high attainments in specific aspects of reading can be achieved at the cost of developing negative attitudes. Excessive drilling in word-recognition could lead to such a situation. Attitudes to reading are as important as attainments.

Measurement is the assigning of numbers to objects or events, according to rules. It is one means of helping us be explicit concerning our activities. Teachers are applied social scientists. As such, we have a professional responsibility to describe, predict and intervene in the learner's reading acquisition processes where this will benefit the student. Reading tests and assessment techniques are valuable means whereby our conceptualisations of the reading process and its development can be made explicit and the validity of our insights, predictions and interventions tested.

The measurement of a person's height tells us something about the individual. Knowledge of his/her weight elaborates the picture. The more dimensions or traits on which we have information, the fuller our description. The uniqueness of the individual reader can be described in terms of his/her relative position on a large number of unidimensional traits. The relationships between the traits must also be known. Attitudes towards reading have to be included if our descriptions are to be adequate.

The notion that attitude scales describe only static products of the reading curriculum (in its widest sense) rather than the dynamics of the reading process can be partially rebutted. Process is always inferred from products. Attitudes to reading are inferred from behaviours of various types. The closer and more detailed the observation of products, the more likely are the inferences about processes to be helpful in understanding the complexities of reading and its development.

The teaching of reading is also an art. Phillip Larkin has written a poem entitled 'A Study of Reading Habits'. In three short verses he vividly portrays one individual's changing perceptions concerning the value of reading. Larkin's poem is a salutory warning to all who are interested in measuring the variety and changes in attitude to reading. The endeavour is complex. It is also worthwhile.

Whilst recognising the theoretical and practical importance of the attitudes towards reading held by significant others (e.g. friends, parents and teachers), the focus of this paper is restricted to attitudes to reading held by students at the primary and secondary stages of education.

Reading

Reading is a complex developmental process. The purposes in reading of the fluent reader are not necessarily the same as those of the learner. Typically, abilities, interests and attitudes differentiate as the individual matures. Attitudes to reading may depend on the personal significance of particular written material. The accountant may be fascinated by the technical detail of a Finance Bill. Its content can be professionally and personally of crucial importance. This will not be the case for all equally competent readers. We read for different purposes. These purposes become differentiated and related to particular needs and contents. Thus, for example, Arts and Science students specialising in different fields of study may be equally competent readers but have preferences for particular fields and even authors within fields. Their attitudes to reading may be equivalent insofar as a score on an attitude to reading scale is concerned. If, however, they read different materials, their attitudes to reading cannot be adequately considered without reference to their preferred content. Interest in a particular activity can affect the appeal of written material.

At the earlier stages in learning to read, it may be that a student's attitudes to reading and interests are less clearly differentiated. The evidence concerning the popularity of different types of written material does suggest that interests in particular types of content do develop as readers become more proficient.

Attitudes to reading

Most local education authorities (LEAs) system-atically test attainment in reading (Gipps et al., 1983; Pumfrey, 1984). The same cannot be said for attitudes towards reading. In part this is because our measures of attitudes to reading reflect the situation concerning the measurement of attitudes in general. Such tests, scales and techniques as we have are less reliable and less valid, according to conventional test theory criteria, than reading attainment tests.

Difficulties arise in this area of measurement for many reasons. An initial step in developing a measuring instrument is to specify the nature of the attribute to be measured. In relation to reading, there has often been an implicit assumption that students' attitudes towards reading could be considered as situated at a point on a continuum ranging from positive to negative; that the construct was unidimensional and susceptible to measurement on a bipolar continuum. Many of the earlier attempts to

118

construct scales in this area suffer from this conceptual limitation.

Workers involved in the field of attitude formation and change distinguish cognitive, affective and conative aspects of attitudes, (Triandis, 1971; Fishbein and Ajzen, 1975). Attitudes to reading can be construed in terms of this model (and other more complex ones). The influence of such models can be seen in some of the techniques and scales listed in Tables 1 and 2.

Table 1: Techniques that have been used to describe students' attitudes to reading

A. Observational approaches:

1. Direct observation by adult of student behaviours in relation to reading materials in educational settings.

2. Checklists of reading-related behaviours from which attitude to reading is inferred.

B. Self-report techniques:

1. Method of paired comparisons
2. Method of equal appearing intervals
3. Method of successive intervals
4. Method of summated ratings
5. Scalogram analysis
6. Adapted Rasch scaling
7. Factorial scales
8. Projective techniques
9. Semantic differential techniques
10. Repertory grid techniques

Attitudes to reading can be conceptualised so as to include 'the individual's feelings, beliefs and values as elicited in relation to reading ...experiences. In this way, attitude is seen as multidimensional and dynamic rather than unitary and static' (Ewing and Johnstone, 1981). The task

Table 2: Some Recent Attitude to Reading Scales

Instrument	Reference	
Attitude Scales (Primary Survey)	APU, 1982a (UK)	Attitudes towards aspects of reading 1. Pleasure in independent, extended reading 2. Preference for reading as a leisure activity 3. Preference for factual reading (7 items) 4. Reluctance towards extended reading 5. Preference for reading aloud rather than to self 6. Dislike of reading aloud 7. Reading for self-improvement
Attitude Scales (Secondary Survey)	APU, 1983 (UK)	Attitudes towards aspects of reading 1. Pleasure in independent, extended reading 2. Reluctance towards extended reading 3. Reading for self-improvement 4. Preference for factual reading. 5. Attitude towards reading aloud. 6. Attitude towards school activities associated with reading
Attitudes to Reading Test 1 (situational) ATR 1	Ewing and Johnstone, 1981 (UK)	Attitudes to reading (situational) A. Affective (how much do I like this kind of reading?) B. Instrumental (how useful is this reading to me?) C. Evaluative (how important is this for me at school?)
Attitude to Reading (global) ATR2	Ewing and Johnstone, 1981 (UK)	Attitudes to reading (global)
Reading Attitude Scales	Lewis and Teale, 1980, 1982; Teale and Lewis, 1980 (Australia/USA)	Attitudes to reading * I. Individual development factor II. Utilitarian factor III. Enjoyment
	Lewis and Teale, undated. (Australia/USA)	Attitudes to reading * I. Individual development factor II. Utilitarian factor (School) III. Utilitarian factor (Work) IV. Enjoyment

* 'The three-factor scales currently have more data to support them than the four-factor. But we have evidence in a study from 1980 that the Utilitarian (Work) factor could be distinguished from the Utilitarian (School) factor.' (Personal communication, 1984)

of operationally defining the field requires considerable empirical research (Rye, 1983).

It must also be remembered that an attitude towards an activity is, in part, a function of the alternative activities that are simultaneously open to the individual. In some situations reading will be viewed more or less favourably, dependent on the options available. In solitary confinement, reading could be highly valued. At a holiday camp it might not be as positively viewed. Given a television set and a variety of reading materials, on which activity would more time be invested? Premack's pre-potent response hypothesis must be borne in mind if we are not to be led into a spurious simplification. In essence, this reminds us of the importance of an ethnomethodological approach to the measurement of attitudes.

The 'Affective Domain Special Interest Group' of the International Reading Association publishes twice-yearly the **ADSIG Journal**. It accepts articles related to the affective aspects of reading. Theoretical, experimental, descriptive and review papers are included. Descriptions of innovative practices are also welcome. The journal is an indication of interest in this particular field.

Useful surveys describing the issues involved in measuring attitudes to reading and describing specific scales and other assessment procedures are available (Deck and Jackson, 1976; Alexander and Filler, 1977; Summers, 1977; Henerson et al., 1978; Ewing and Johnstone, 1981; Epstein, 1981).

Assessment techniques

A range of different techniques for measuring attitudes have been developed. Some of the more important recent ones are listed in Table 2. Two major approaches can be distinguished. The first is based on observation of students; the second on

121

self-report techniques. The ability to describe attitudes to reading depends on observations obtained in three different ways and known, respectively, as L-data, Q-data and T-data. L-data refers to behaviour observed, recorded or rated in a specified live environmental context. Q-data refers to questionnaire self-evaluations and T-data has been defined as test data based on a 'standard, portable, stimulus situation in which the student's behaviour is measured without the student being aware' (Cattell and Warburton, 1967). These authors point to the dangerous attraction to research workers of 'regression to the questionnaire'. Although their own work was oriented towards the development of a taxonomy of objective tests, the pitfalls to which they point should be noted by anyone intending to work in the field of attitudes to reading. In essence, the relationship between self-report of attitudes to reading and reading behaviours can be modified by many influences. For example, the subtle pressures that can operate to make the student 'fake good' when answering a self-report questionnaire, may be very potent in certain circumstances, enhancing or reducing the correlations with other indices.

The techniques listed above have been clearly described in publications (Edwards, 1957; Oppenheim, 1972, Henerson et al., 1978). The reader will find that these books also provide guidance concerning other work in this area.

One important sub-set of observational approaches, is the use of what are described as 'unobtrusive' measures. These refer to nonreactive techniques designed to have minimal effects on the phenomena they are being used to measure (Epstein, 1981). These could include the issue and frequency of use of school library tickets, purchase of reading materials through a school book club and membership of a local library. The use of a Reading Record Form as used in the Bradford 'Book Flood' Experiment, whilst hardly being unobtrusive, was one way of monitoring the degree and variety of students' involvement with books over a three-year period (Ingham, 1982). Attendance at a remedial reading centre could also be used as an unobtrusive measure. However, the empirical links between such indices and students' attainments in reading still present only a correlation. The causal relationships involved remain obscure.

A strong case has been made for a multi-measure approach in which complementary sources of data are used (Summers, 1977; Ewing and Johnstone, 1981; Lewis and Teale, 1980, 1982). The thesis here presented is that an adequate assessment of attitudes to reading requires the use of data obtained from observational and self-report sources.

Some recently developed scales

A recent survey of 199 reading tests and assessment techniques contains descriptions of eight British and nine American instruments designed to measure attitudes to reading (Pumfrey, 1985). Several of these instruments contain a number of scales measuring different aspects of the attitude to reading. The most recently developed ones are shown in Table 2. They represent a move towards recognising the complexities involved.

The Assessment of Performance Unit of the Department of Education and Science (APU) is involved in monitoring the attainments and attitudes that contribute to literacy (cf. Thornton, this volume). Building on work done in 1979, in 1980 pupils' attitudes to reading were elicited using two questionnaires each containing ten sentence-completion items and 40 statements for pupils to respond to on a five point scale. The pattern of scales subsequently identified was very similar to that obtained earlier, with some slight amendments. Thus references to fictional reading were linked to pleasure in independent, extended reading (Scale 1). References to leisure activities such as reading, television, comics and periodicals appeared as a discrete factor. Attitudes to reading aloud split into two factors. One concerned dislike of such activity and the other a preference for reading aloud rather than silent reading on one's own (APU, 1982a). In the scales, each item is a positive statement requiring a response on a 0-4 scale.

Significant sex differences were found on scales 1, 2, and 3. The girls obtained higher mean scores on scales 1 and 2; boys obtained a higher mean score on scale 3.

The construct validity of the scales rests largely on the extensive preliminary work done in exploring the domain, and on the factor analyses carried out. The internal consistency reliability coefficients (Cronbach's alpha) ranged from 0.42 to 0.83. Correlations of the seven scales with reading attainments ranged from -0.11 to -0.45. All of these were significantly greater than zero ($p < 0.001$) except for scales 4 and 6 where $p < 0.012$ and $p < 0.02$ respectively.

A number of technical points concerning the construction of the scales are unclear from the report. The factor-analytic methods used and the inter-correlations of the scales are two important points in question. Such consid-erations affect the interpretation of the results obtained. The scales also have the weaknesses of being relatively short, with an associated tendency to unreliability. The 'visibility' of what is being assessed, coupled with the social desirability of responses in given directions, suggests that the tendency to 'fake good' might operate.

The information on attitudes to reading and other aspects of literacy presented in the three

APU Primary Surveys published to date is one of the most valuable British sources readily available to teachers (APU, 1981, 1982a, 1984).

The APU's work in the secondary school field has also yielded valuable information on attitudes to reading. The 1983 report describes a similar strategy to that used in the Primary Surveys outlined earlier. Factor analyses of data based on a stratified random sample of 1,091 15-year-old pupils attending 282 schools led to the identification of the six scales shown in Table 2 (APU, 1983).

Sex differences with the girls obtaining the more positive scores, were found in scales 1, 3 and 6. The reverse applied to scales 2 and 4. On scale 5 there was no significant sex difference.

As with the Primary Scales, construct validity rests on the extensive preliminary work (APU, 1982b) and on the factor analyses carried out. Internal consistency reliabilities based on Cronbach's alpha ranged from 0.77 to 0.91. Four of the scales, numbers 1-4, correlated significantly with reading performance scores.

As with the Primary Scales, major weaknesses include 'visibility' and the possibility of social desirability response set occurring. Technical details of factor analyses and of relationships between the scales are not given.

Despite such comments, these two APU Secondary Surveys are one of the most important and useful British sources concerned with attitudes to reading and other aspects of literacy available in this country.

The Scottish Education Department funded an extensive research project that led to the construction and validation of attitudes to reading tests covering both primary and secondary school age groups (Ewing and Johnstone, 1981).

After extensive pilot studies, it was decided to use Likert scaling based on five-point responses to items in devising what the authors called a 'Situation-specific affective/evaluative attitude scale'. Twenty reading situations, mainly, but not exclusively, referring to classroom reading activities were compiled after consultations with pupils and teachers. Three forms of the same 20 items were prepared varying in item sequence and the three aspects of reading identified as pertinent by the researchers (see Table 1). The items were tried out on 5,911 pupils attending a representative sample of 19 primary and five secondary schools in the Tayside region. About 16 per cent of the primary sample and 10 per cent of the secondary sample returned incomplete or unclear responses. This introduces an unquantified potential source of error variance, but is a commonly occurring phenomenon in such research. The data were factor analysed in various ways. The most meaningful analyses utilised 'principal factoring, without iteration, rotated orthogonally using the equimax technique' to produce simplification (op. cit. p.42). In the event, the analysis of all 60 variables for all pupils gave a confused picture. The clearest analyses resulted from taking the a priori division of attitude into affect, instrumental and evaluative aspects. As the authors carefully explain, these three factors are themselves complex and interrelated. For a better appreciation of such considerations the potential user of the scales should consult the manual. It is concluded that the final form of the scales may retain only the 'like' and 'useful' judgements and exclude the 'important' scale. This has now been done (Ewing, personal communication, 1983).

The reported split-half reliabilities of the three scales were 0.74, 0.79 and 0.85 at the primary school level and 0.80, 0.84 and 0.87 at the secondary school level. Validities were assessed using criterion-group comparisons. The

ATR1 scales were constructed simultaneously with ATR2. The latter scale contains 18 items, nine positive and nine negative, and was devised to assess a global attitude towards reading. Ratings are summated to give a range of scores. From a sample of 2,923 pupils at age levels P5, P7, S2 and S4, split-half internal consistency reliability coefficients of 0.80 and 0.88 are reported for the primary and secondary samples respectively.

On ATR2, primary pupils obtained higher (more favourable) mean scores than secondary school pupils and girls had, on average, more positive attitudes than boys. However, the factor analyses that were carried out failed to produce support for the notion that ATR2 did assess a global characteristic. Three different factors were identified. Factor 1 (nine items) is interpreted as characterising the non-involved reader. Factor 2 (six items) taps a 'pleasure or enthusiasm factor'. Factor 3 (three items) is interpreted as a 'utilitarian or learning, factor'. This finding underlines the complexity of attitudes to reading, as did the related work on ATR1.

Presumably work will continue with both ATR1 and ATR2. The manual contains details of the theorising, the experimental techniques, analysis and validation that do indicate promising avenues for further research and classroom application. Some apparent cul-de-sacs are also indicated.

The work in Australia and subsequently in the USA of Lewis and Teale has a close affinity to that done in Scotland. Initially, the former co-workers' research was concerned with secondary school pupils, but has, more recently, been demonstrated to be applicable to primary school pupils also (Lewis and Teale, 1980, 1982). Teale, in reviewing the reading attitudes-reading attainments relationship points to the confusing picture obtained from a range of studies. 'It is at this point that I wish I could say "In the remainder of this paper, I would like to proffer a principled paradigm by which the various theories and results can be synthesised, such that an elegant conceptual account of the attitude-achievement interconnection is provided". Unfortunately, I have no such paradigm.'

They point to the absence of an adequately articulated theoretical basis for the development of attitudes to reading scales. More importantly, they have begun to develop such a model.

They point to the different purposes involved in the reader's relation to textual materials. From earlier work on attitudes in general, they have developed a model that attempts to incorporate cognitive (beliefs about reading), affective (feelings about reading) and conative (intentions/behaviours) components of attitudes toward reading. This has led them to construct two conceptually related batteries of scales. The first contains three scales. The first scale, Individual Development, measures the extent to which students value reading as a means of individual development. The second, Utilitarian, measures students' valuing of reading as a means of achieving success in educational or occupational terms. The third construct, Enjoyment, is affective in nature. The three are seen as crucially important cognitive and affective components of their model.

The construct validity of the scales is supported by factor analyses of the scores of 14- and 18-year-old pupils carried out in 1978 and 1979. A satisfactory degree of internal consistency has been demonstrated. Using 50 and 43 of the 14- and 18-year-old pupils respectively, test-retest reliabilities, over a two to four week period, of 0.72 and 0.90 are reported. Validity is attested to in that students nominated by their peers as 'high' or 'low' on the scales, differed in the predicted directions. The correlation between the scales are such that the authors claim that they have identified 'three potentially distinguishable constructs within reading attitudes' for the sample tested (Lewis and Teale, 1980). They have subsequently tested the constructs using 10- and 12-year-old Australian students. Of their results, they say that the correlations between the scales are modest but 'sufficiently small to suggest that the constructs should no longer be combined by researchers to form one scale' (Lewis and Teale, op. cit.). When analysed by age group, it is claimed that the Enjoyment items load on one factor but that the pattern for the remaining items make it impossible to interpret the results in terms of the loadings found at the secondary school stage. It is argued that this may be one consequence of the younger children's narrower field of experience in relation to reading activities. They do not appear to discriminate between valuing reading for personal individual development and valuing it for its utilitarian purposes. Initial analyses of work carried out in England in the autumn of 1984 in assessing the attitudes towards reading of 11- to 12-year-old pupils at a comprehensive school suggests that differentiation of attitudes to reading by this age is far from clear cut (Eltrincham et al., 1985).

A study carried out by Teale in 1980 is said to support the existence of four factors. The scales used to measure these each contain seven items. One of the authors has said that the Utilitarian factor split into two: one related to school endeavours and one to occupational ones (Teale, personal communication, 1984).

Ways forward

The major barriers to advances in this field are:

1. The need for an explicit conceptual and

theoretical framework within which attitudes towards reading can be set;

2. Empirical studies using L, Q and, if possible, T data;

3. Greater availability of information on the validities of attitude to reading scales;

4. An enhanced professional awareness of the weaknesses of self-report questionnaires;

5. Sensitivity to the effects of scale 'visibility' and the social desirability set;

6. School-based work on conditions conducive to changing attitudes to reading in a positive direction;

7. An awareness of the importance of situational contexts, the form and content of the textual material and the reader's purposes and interests.

Conclusion

Is the search for valid assessments of attitudes to reading worthwhile? Is the endeavour no more than an infant of fashion, an educational bandwaggon: or could it lead to an important breakthrough? Will such work help us enable students attain the 'double-barrelled' educational objective specified at the start of this paper? Doubters may cite the words of Lewis Carroll in warning: 'When I use a word,' Humpty Dumpty said in a rather scornful tone, 'it means just what I choose it to mean, neither more nor less'. 'The question is,' said Alice 'whether you can make words mean so many different things'. 'The question is,' said Humpty Dumpty, 'which is to be the master?'

From the evidence presented, attitudes towards reading are currently more adequately conceived and measured than 20 years ago. Progress has been made. More can be achieved.

References

Alexander, J.E. and Filler, R.C. (1977) Attitudes and Reading Newark, Delaware: International Reading Association (2nd printing).

APU (1981) Language Performance in Schools: Primary Survey Report No. 1. London: HMSO.

APU (1982a) Language Performance in Schools: Primary Survey Report No. 2. London: HMSO.

APU (1982b) Language Performance in Schools: Secondary Survey Report No. 1. London: HMSO.

APU (1983) Language Performance in Schools: Secondary Survey Report No. 2. London: HMSO.

APU (1984) Language Performance in Schools: 1982 Primary Survey Report. London: DES.

Cattell, R.B. and Warburton, F.W. (1967) Objective Personality and Motivation Tests: a theoretical introduction and practical compendium. Urbana: University of Illinois Press.

Deck, D. and Jackson, B.J. (1976) Measuring Attitudes Towards Reading in Large Scale Assessment. Pennsylvania: Pennsylvania State University, Centre for Cooperative Research with Schools.

Edwards, A.L. (1957) Techniques of Attitude Scale Construction. New York: Appleton-Century-Crofts.

Eltringham, J., Fromings, J., Kavanagh, R., Shackleton, K. and Wickham, D. (1985) Attitudes towards reading of 11-year-old to 12-year-old pupils in a comprehensive school. Unpublished Test Construction Exercise. Manchester:

University of Manchester Department of Education.

Epstein, I. (1981) Measuring Attitudes toward Reading. Princeton: Educational Testing Service.

Ewing, J.M. and Johnstone, M. (1981) Attitudes to Reading: measurement and classification within a curricular structure. Dundee: Dundee College of Education.

Fishbein, M. and Ajzen, I. (1975) Belief, Attitude, Intention and Behaviour. Reading, Massachusetts: Addison-Wesley.

Gipps, C., Steadman, S., Blackstone, T. and Stierer, B. (1983) Testing Children: standard-ised testing in local education authorities and schools. London: Heinemann Educational.

Henerson, M.E., Morris, L.L. and Fitz-Gibbon, C.T. (1978) How to Measure Attitudes. London: Sage.

Ingham, J. (1982) Books and Reading Development: the Bradford 'Book Flood' experiment. London: Heinemann Educational (2nd Edn.).

Lewis, R. and Teale W.H. (1980) Another look at secondary school students' attitudes toward reading. Journal of Reading Behavior, 12 (3) 187-201.

Lewis, R. and Teale, W.H. (1982) Primary school students' attitudes towards reading. Journal of Research in Reading, 5 (2) 113-122.

Oppenheim, A.N. (1972) Questionnaire Design and Attitude Measurement. London: Heinemann Educational.

Pumfrey, P.D. (1984) Monitoring the reading attainments of ethnic minority children: national survey of LEA practices. New Community, 11 (3) 268-277.

Pumfrey, P.D. (1985) Reading: tests and assessment techniques. Sevenoaks: Hodder and Stoughton.

Rye, J. (1983) The importance of attitude; some implications. Reading, 17 (1) 13-22.

Summers, E.G. (1977) Instruments for assessing reading attitudes: a review of research and a bibliography. Journal of Reading Behavior, 9, 137-165.

Teale, W.H. (undated) Reading attitudes and reading achievement: domain-specific relations? (unpublished ms).

Teale, W.H. and Lewis, R. (1980) The nature of students' attitudes towards reading: implications for reading instruction and curriculum development. In T. Bessell-Browne et al. (Eds.) Reading into the 80's. Perth: Australian Reading Association.

Triandis, H.C. (1971) Attitude and Attitude Change. New York: Wiley.

Further Reading

Bennie, F. (1973) Pupils' attitudes to individually-prescribed laboratory programs. Journal of Reading, November, 108-112

Estes, T.H., Roettger, D.M., Johnstone, J.P. and Richards, H.C. (1976) Estes Attitude Scales: elementary form. Charlottesville: Virginia Research Associates.

Heathington, B.S. and Alexander, J.E. (1978) A child-based observation checklist to assess attitudes towards reading. Reading Teacher, 31, 769-771.

Howlet, N. and Weintraub, S. (1979) Instructional Procedures. In R.C. Calfee and P.A. Drum (Eds.) Teaching Reading in Compensatory Classes. Newark, Delaware: International Reading Association.

Hunter-Grundin, E. and Hunter-Grundin, H.U. (1980) Hunter-Grundin Literacy Profiles. High Wycombe: The Test Agency.

Kelly, G.A. (1955) Psychology of Personal Constructs. New York: Norton.

Kennedy, L.D. and Halinski, R.S. (1975) Measuring attitudes: an extra dimension. Journal of Reading, 18 (7) 518-522.

Mickulecky, L.J., Shanklin, N.L. and Caverly, D.C. (1979) Adult reading habits, attitudes and motivations: a cross-sectional study. Monograph in Language and Reading Studies, No. 2. Indiana: Indiana University School of Education.

Monson, D. and McClenathan, D. (Eds.) (1980) Developing Active Readers: ideas for parents, teachers and librarians. Newark, Delaware: International Reading Association.

Osgood, C.E., Suci, G.J. and Tannenbaum, P.H. (1957) The Measurement of Meaning. Urbana: University of Illinois Press.

Pennsylvania State Department of Education (1975) Attitudes Toward Reading Scale. ERIC Document ED120647.

Pumfrey, P.D. and Dixon, E. (1970) Junior children's attitude to reading: comments on three measuring instruments. Reading, 4 (2) 19-26.

Remmers, H.H. (1960) Generalised Attitude Scales. In M.E. Shaw and J.M. Wright (1967) Scales for the Measurement of Attitudes. New York: McGraw-Hill.

Roettger, D., Szymezuk, M. and Millard, J. (1979)
Validation of a reading attitude scale for
elementary students and an investigation into the
relationship between attitude and attainment.
Journal of Educational Research, 72, 138-142.

Rowell, G.C. (1972) An attitude scale for
reading. The Reading Teacher, 25, 442-447.

Tullock-Rhody, R. and Alexander, J.E. (1980) A
scale for assessing attitudes towards reading in
secondary schools. Journal of Reading, 23, 609-
614.

Turner, C.J. and Smith, J.K. (1982) Traditional
versus Rasch scaling of aggregate data in a
multitrait-multimethod matrix. Measurement and
Evaluation in Guidance, 14 (4) 180-186.

Vaughan, J.L. Jnr. (1977) A scale to measure
attitudes towards teaching reading in content
classrooms. Journal of Reading, 20 (7) 605-609.

Eye Movement Monitoring in Diagnosis and Assessment

A. K. Pugh

Eye movement monitoring of reading has the advantage over many testing procedures that it does not impose a particular type of reading on the reader, since samples can be taken of the reading of almost any text read for almost any purpose. However, eye movement monitoring has been little used outside research applications in Britain where it has until recently been seen as of little interest to teachers and of limited application in testing. This view has obtained even though eye movement records have been made in reading clinics in the United States over a long period (from the 1920s to the present).

In fact, eye movement research has not had a good press and its history is uneven (Kolers, 1976; Pugh, 1984). Although it held out huge promise for research in reading, as Huey (1908) discerned, we have long left those 'giddy days when eye movements seemed to some the key to the soul' (as Coles, 1983, puts it). Even the more modest appraisal of Rayner, (1983) that eye movements are not the only way to study reading, but that they are a good way, would meet with some reservations.

In part, doubts over eye movement monitoring have stemmed from technical problems with equipment. In part, the problem has been in integration and application of what has been found. An extreme example of misapplication is the pseudo scientific nonsense one finds in some classes in speed reading which include advice and exercises to improve eye movements (see Pugh, 1978).

Nevertheless, despite the dubious antecedents and the technical difficulties, eye movements have again in the last few years become of interest to cognitive psychologists engaged in studying the reading process and to other researchers who are more concerned with clarifying the sources of the profound difficulty which some children encounter specifically with reading and writing. Several volumes, including the important collection edited by Rayner (1983), attest to this renewed interest.

The reasons for the resurgence of interest are varied. They include the following:

1. Technical advances in electronic equipment which make for more accurate, and mort readily interpretable data;

2. The movement towards 'ecological validity', real tests and natural situations in cognitive psychology, contrasted with the 'old' psycho-linguistics;

3. The new respectability achieved by dyslexia as it has come to be studied by reputable academic psychologists (ignoring or ignorant of the reading establishment's position on this term).

In recent years, and particularly in Britain, a number of researchers have increasingly recognised that visual factors may very likely be associated with severe reading difficulty among those who cope relatively better with other subjects or skills than they do with reading. Eye movement monitoring has been used in attempting to ascertain the characteristics of such readers and these studies have employed, and often suggested, techniques which can be used in diagnosis.

The definition of what unusual behaviours we are testing for remains not entirely agreed, yet the work is of sufficient importance for a brief review to be offered in this paper of some relevant British work.

Dyslexia and eye movements

Although earlier researchers, such as Buswell (1922), Tinker, (1965) and Vernon (1931, 1971) examined the relationship between eye movement patterns and problems in reading, researchers into dyslexia have only relatively recently become interested in monitoring eye movements even though they have long been aware that visual problems may be implicated. In fact, despite the longstanding recognition (or hypothesis) that neurological factors are involved in dyslexia (Hynd and Hynd, 1984 give a useful review), much of the research effort seems to have been devoted to a definition of dyslexia. Thus there has not been a good basis for eye movement studies where it helps if one knows what kind of pattern one is looking for. Certainly there are very few studies of eye movements in relation to studies of reading generally, and of visual behaviour in relation to studies on severe problems in reading.

This view is borne out by examination of the volumes of the **Summary of Investigation related to Reading** edited by Sam Weintraub and others for the International Reading Association. The studies there are mainly North American but the same seems true for Europe. Of 50 studies of dyslexia in Germany reviewed by Valtin (1984) only two were on eye movements. These, which examined patterns in reading, Valtin criticises for their lack of theoretical basis and therapeutic application.

However, enthusiastic work by George Pavlidis led to a series of papers beginning in 1978 (reviewed in Pavlidis, 1983) which brought out the possibility that the key to the problems of dyslexia would be found by analysis of the eye movements of dyslexics. Moreover, Pavlidis attacked the use of tests for diagnosis whose results were used to look for CA/RA discrepancy and proposed instead that to diagnose properly one should examine the eye movements of suspected dyslexics when reading and when following a sequence of lights. Pavlidis has not produced quantified results generally but has given individual pen records and illustrative data. He has claimed to have identified certain characteristics unique to dyslexics including clusters of regressions, unclear line ends and others.

There is a difficulty with these results, even if they are accepted, in that we are unsure whether the reading problem is central or peripheral - a very old argument in eye movement studies which is crucial for interpretation of their results and hence to acting on them. Briefly, if the problem is peripheral, training the eyes may help, but if it is central it is less clear what should be treated. However, one may not accept Pavlidis' results which are based on data from small samples and chosen according to questionable criteria. Above all, they may fail to find acceptance because the differences between the eye movements of dyslexics and others are not clear. Pollatsek (1983) as discussant of Pavlidis (1983) notes that he cannot discern the claimed qualitative difference in pattern. Other studies such as those reported and cited in Rayner (1983) lend some support to the view that the eye movements of dyslexics are unusual, but it remains to be clarified whether their eye movement patterns are peculiar to them and, if so, precisely what the characteristics of these patterns are.

Problems of binocular vision

Most studies have employed monocular recording - often only of the horizontal. Yet, there is a well-established view that eye dominance may be related to reading difficulty. In general, studies of this have employed 'static' tests of vision - rather than dynamic tests of visual behaviour in reading - largely, one suspects, because of the lack of equipment for monitoring binocular vision in reading. Yet, confusion of left and right hand has been correlated in many studies with reading problems, so the incidence of confusion in visual coordination seems likely. It is established (e.g. Jones and Lee, 1981) that two-eyed performance on various tasks is much superior (at least in results) to monocular vision though head movement can help to overcome the difficulties of looking with one eye in certain tasks.

Another enthusiastic researcher with a 'clinical' background is Ron Grant, who has, partly in association with Charles Bedwell, examined visual factors related to reading difficulty. As with Pavlidis, there are so far some problems of sample size and also considerable difficulties in interpretation. Nevertheless, Grant has practitioner experience (as an advisory remedial teacher) of diagnosis. One kind of difficulty he has been particularly interested in is convergence/divergence and Grant and Peters (1981) offer a discussion of the problem as well as suggestions for remediation. Elsewhere, Grant (1984) provides examples of eye movement patterns which he considers typical of a number of kinds of reading problem. The data are suggestive only but they serve to indicate more clearly than Pavlidis and others the kind of problem which may be looked for in the eye movement records.

Binocular vision need not be tested dynamically. Grant himself has devised a simple method using polarised spectacles for assessing the dominant eye for reading, though it needs to be said that in our experience it is not a very consistent method. This is probably because distance from the text has a strong effect on what is reported, but it is hard to keep that distance constant at the preferred distance for reading.

A much more sophisticated test is the Dunlop test, as used by Stein and Fowler (1982) in their studies of eye dominance and dyslexia. They found unstable ocular dominance in 63 per cent of the 80 children referred with reading problems to the Royal Berkshire Hospital, but in only one out of 80 of their normal subjects. One suggestion from the study which has had some support is that occlusion of one eye over a fairly lengthy period will help to rectify the instability and thus contribute to remedying the dyslexia. However, Newman et al. (1985), have carried out an unusually exact replication of the study of Stein and Fowler. The main difference between the studies seems to be that although dyslexia was defined in both as 18 months behind chronological age in reading or spelling, Newman et al. drew all their subjects from normal schools. Stein and Fowler, however, compared referred dyslexics with controls. Among their 298 subjects, aged 7 to 11, Newman et al. found no significant relationship between established ocular dominance and dyslexia. Although they agreed with Stein and Fowler on the incidence of ocular instability among dyslexics, Newman et al. found a similar incidence among their other subjects.

It may seem that Stein and Fowler made a classical error, for, in studies on a similar topic, it has been long recognised (e.g. Vernon, 1971, p.138) that studies of school populations have not found a relationship between handedness or eyedness and reading problems whereas studies of referred populations have shown large numbers with mixed handedness - often with directional confusion. Harris and Sipay (1980, p.290) cite several relevant references. However, this point about referred samples would not explain why Newman et al. found a similar level of ocular instability among all their subjects to that found by Stein and Fowler among their dyslexics only.

The argument here is not an esoteric one about research methodologies, for the occlusion of one eye by wearing modified spectacles is a conspicuous treatment which singles out those receiving it. It is also a dubious treatment for reasons which emerge from our own studies as well as those from that of Newman et al.

If few studies have considered binocular vision, many fewer have examined eye movements related to head movements in reading. Our studies (e.g. Netchine, Pugh and Guihou, 1985) include current work comparing the head movements of French 9- to 10-year-olds with those of English children of a similar age, and taking into account factors such as preferred eye, functional and neurological laterality, difficulty of text.

Interestingly, the preliminary results show considerably greater incidence of head movement in French children. Negative correlations were found between head movement and reading ability in both the French group and the English group and we found cases of head movements which almost exactly replace eye movements (a difficult feat given the weight of the head, but reported also in Netchine, Solomon and Guihou, 1981; Netchine et al., 1983). Inspection of the recordings revealed few instances of apparent divergence/convergence problems in our sample of 34 9- to 10-year-olds, and only slight evidence of a tendency to 'use' one eye in preference to the other or to switch from one preferred eye at one point to another preferred eye at another (perhaps because of position in relation to the text). We should not yet expect, as the work is in progress, to be in a position to lay down clear guidelines for diagnosis, but we are concerned that we do not clearly find on inspection (by experienced researchers) the clear qualitative differences which Grant and Pavlidis allude to.

Perhaps their problem is that (as with Stein and Fowler) they are dealing with referred samples. However, the problem could be more serious than that. In another study, also in progress, I have examined the effects on actual reading of the occlusion of one eye which Stein and Fowler recommend and which appears to be practised by some opthalmologists. For this, a trial was given of reading with both eyes of a passage from a test similar to the Neale test. Then one passage of the Neale test was read with both eyes and then another passage with one eye occluded with blue tinted plastic. Some practice in reading with one eye was then given and a further recording taken with the same eye occluded as before. Of the 16 subjects (8 boys, 8 girls aged 9 to 10; RQ range 78-93) the majority showed no preferred eye on testing with Grant's polarised spectacles, referred to earlier. However, as all the subjects were right handed it was somewhat arbitrarily decided to cover the left eye. One subject showed possible problems of instability with convergence of the eyes. Otherwise the reading seemed to be in a fairly normal pattern except in five cases. There the expected result was not obtained, i.e. it was not found that the occluded eye did markedly less work as judged by fixation frequency and sharpness of steps. (Direct comparisons of size for the two ages could not be made for technical reasons with analogue equipment without considerable delays in setting up and there is a need to restrain head movement). The five were retested (as was the one with possible convergence/divergence problems) and it was found again in three of the cases that the covered eye (now the right) appeared to be doing as much work, or more than when it was not covered. In other words we obtained some very convincing records of eye movement in reading from an eye which could not possibly see clearly enough to read at all. This questions the interpretation of much eye movement data but is particularly worrying for those studies which rely on monitoring only movements from one eye, as most research has done.

Conclusions

Where does this leave eye movements as a diagnostic or assessment technique? Most strikingly, it suggests that there may be a danger of jumping to conclusions when a good deal of work needs to be done. This is not an argument for not doing the work, for eye movement monitoring has advantages mentioned earlier of providing a means of studying the reading of normal text under relatively normal conditions.

As eye movements can more easily and cheaply be recorded and analysed, there is opportunity to examine more carefully and fully the patterns of eye movements in large samples (as Newman et al., personal communication, are now doing). There remain problems of interpretation since it is not established to what extent the eye mirrors what the mind is concerned with and the complex visual/mental interaction in reading text has to be explored more fully. Also, the connection between head movement and eye movement warrants much further attention, especially if we (Netchine, Pugh and Guihou, 1985) are correct in suggesting that preferred style of head movement down a page may be associated with apparent changes in preferred eye (which might be mistaken for mixed dominance in the child). Finally, there is a case for studies (and diagnostic procedures) which take account not only of head and eye movements but which also monitor subvocal activity, and, perhaps, arousal (although interpretation of data from skin response techniques is justifiably debated).

The definitions of reading implicit in many approaches to assessment are inadequate but it is hard to see how they can be changed without more knowledge about what occurs in normal reading. This is the argument for more (pure) research of course. More practically, it does seem likely that identifiable visual and other physical symptoms (if not causes) can and will be found in those who have problems with reading. This will help both diagnosis and remediation. Thus, although the interpretation of eye movement recordings is not straightforward, it would seem that they can make an important contribution to diagnosis and assessment of reading. For the moment, however, interpretation and prescriptions should be treated with caution.

References

Buswell, G.T. (1922) Fundamental Reading Habits: a Study of their Development. (Supplementary Education Monograph No. 21) Chicago: University of Chicago.

Coles, P.R. (1983) Methods. In R. Groner et al. (Eds.) Eye Movements and Psychological Functions: international views. Hillsdale, N.J.: Erlbaum.

Grant, R. (1984) Instability of Eye Control. Bognor Regis: VTP Aids.

Grant, R. and Peters, T. (1981) A classroom diagnosis and remediation for reading difficulties related to binocular instability. Remedial Education, 16 (1) 9-17.

Harris, A.J. and Sipay, E.R. (1980) How to Increase Reading Ability (7th Edn.). New York: Longman.

Huey, E.B. (1908) The Psychology and Pedagogy of Reading. New York : Macmillan. (Reprinted Cambridge, Mass.: MIT Press, 1968).

Hynd, G.W. and Hynd, C.R. (1984) Dyslexia: neuroanatomical/neurolinguistic perspectives. Reading Research Quarterly, 19 (4) 482-498.

Jones, R.K. and Lee, D.N. (1981) Why two eyes are better than one: the two views of binocular vision. Journal of Experimental Psychology: Human Perception and Performance, 7, 30-40.

Kolers, P.A. (1976) Buswell's discoveries. In R.A. Monty and J.W. Senders, J.W. (Eds.) Eye Movements and Psychological Processes. Hillsdale, N.J.: Erlbaum.

Netchine, S., Solomon, M. and Guihou, M.C. (1981) Composantes oculaires et cephaliques de l'organisation des deplacements du regard chez les jeunes lecteurs. Psychologie Francaise, 26, 120-124.

Netchine, S. et al. (1983) Retour a la ligne, age des lecteurs et accessibilite au texte. Le Travail Humain, 46, 139-153.

Netchine, S. et al. (1983) Retour a la ligne, age des lecteurs et accessibilite au texte. Le Travail Humain, 46, 139-153.

Netchine, S., Pugh, A.K. and Guihou, M.C. (1985) The organisation of binocular vision in conjunction with head movement in French and English readers of 9 and 10 years. Paper presented to 3rd European Conference on Eye Movements, Dourdan, France, September 1985.

Newman, S. et al. (1985) Ocular dominance, reading and spelling: a reassessment of a measure associated with specific reading difficulties. Journal of Research in Reading, 8 (2) 127-138.

Pavlidis, G.T. (1983) The 'dyslexia syndrome' and its objective diagnosis by erratic eye movements. In K. Rayner, (Ed.) Eye Movements in Reading: perceptual and language processes. New York: Academic Press.

Pollatsek, A. (1983) What can eye movements tell us about dyslexia. In K. Rayner, (Ed.) Eye

Movements in Reading: perceptual and language processes. New York: Academic Press.

Pugh, A.K. (1978) Silent Reading: an introduction to its study and teaching. London: Heinemann.

Pugh, A.K. (1984) Eye-movement studies of readers and text. In A.K. Pugh and J.M. Uljin, (Eds.) Reading for Professional Purposes: studies and practices in native and foreign languages. London: Heinemann.

Rayner, K. (1983) (Ed.) Eye Movements in Reading: perceptual and language processes. New York: Academic Press.

Stein, J.F. and Fowler, S. (1982) Diagnosis of 'dyslexia' by means of a new indicator of eye dominance. British Journal of Opthalmology, 66, 332-336.

Tinker, M.A. (1965) Bases for Effective Reading. Minneapolis : University of Minnesota Press.

Valtin, R. (1984) German studies of dyslexia: implications for education. Journal of Research in Reading, 7 (2) 79-102.

Vernon, M.D. (1931) The Experimental Study of Reading. Cambridge: Cambridge University Press.

Vernon, M.D. (1971) Reading and its Difficulties: a psychological study. Cambridge: Cambridge University Press.

The Use of L1 in Foreign Language Reading Comprehension

Madeline Lutjeharms

If we assume that it is possible to measure foreign language reading comprehension, and we choose a text or texts as a starting-point for this purpose, then what kind of test procedure can be considered appropriate? If we further assume that reading comprehension has already been acquired in the first language, it might be more efficient to test only the difficulties added by the FL-component, i.e. the FL-dependent part of the reading process. This would include strategies like contextual guessing, which is generally thought to improve FL reading comprehension (van Parreren and Schouten-van Parreren, 1981). Appropriate and restricted use of L1 in the FL classroom is no longer taboo. In the receptive method, learners are allowed to talk about the FL texts in the L1, if they find it necessary (Schouten-van Parreren, 1983; cf. Nord, 1980; Davies, 1983).

If L1 has been used consciously to accelerate the learning process, using L1 for testing is probably uncontroversial. L1 patterns tend to predominate unconsciously in any case. This means that some unconscious translating activity may take place (Keil, 1979; Apelt, 1976), especially at the beginning of the learning process. Only errors and error correction will make this process conscious. Deceptive cognates and different structures have to be explicity pointed out (Juhasz, 1970), although use of context to detect them has to be stressed where possible. Of course, use of linguistic analysis, like conscious use of L1, should not be more frequent than necessary (Apelt, 1976).

A problem with the use of L1 for testing FL reading comprehension is that it is perfectly possible to get 'the words without getting the meaning' (Voss, 1984). Translation tests have shown that testees can translate with a kind of 'standard response', i.e. an equivalent word meaning or construction in L1, without use of semantic processing, association between the elements or use of concepts (van Krieken, 1982). To illustrate this we can give an example from one of our tests. The item asked for the translation of the second half of the sentence 'ist das noch freie Mitarbeit oder ist das schon Festanstellung?' A number of testees, all but one with a low test score, translated 'Festan-stellung' as 'Feststellung', which made the sentence nonsensical. The problem in the item is that 'Festanstellung' is translated into Dutch as 'vaste aanstelling', adjective plus noun. Everybody had understood 'freie Mitarbeit' correctly; a Dutch-speaker does not need any knowledge of German to understand this. When the students were asked afterwards to find the right meaning of 'Festanstellung', thinking of what would make sense with 'freie Mitarbeit', all found the right solution. Only the error makes the problem observable. It shows that no attempt had been made at understanding the sentence and that no use of context had been made. The larger context would also have helped.

Interpreters can perform like typists and translate without control of content. Smelcer, Patwardham, Wilson and von Raffles-Engel (1980 p.64) conclude from their pilot study of simultaneous translation 'that translating is governed by a short-term memory. This would adequately explain monitoring and self-correcting. Neither the original text in the source language nor the translation in the target language may reach long-term memory'.

Another well-known experience is to get the meaning, but not the words, an experience happening probably more often in a FL than in L1 (cf. Voss, 1984). As long as the words are still in the short-term memory repetition is possible, but once the information is processed and stored in long-term memory, we can repeat the information, albeit in general and not with the actual words. If mastery of the FL is limited, repetition will only be possible in L1. The FL material has not been stored, although it has been understood. In reading comprehension, this last aspect, the processing of information, is important rather than the actual words or structures. These may, of course, be acquired through experience in the long run. Readers have been found to understand more than they can report (de Beaugrande, 1981). If the information source remains at the disposal of testees, setting them to work with a good idea of what is expected of them, so that they start with a large enough working memory capacity, might improve the test results.

These experiences and the role of L1 in the learning process provide some evidence in favour of a sensible use of L1 in the testing of FL reading comprehension.

The use of L1 for questions and answers is only possible if all testees have the same source language. The fact that most research stems from the USA and from work with testees having different source languages might explain why, in the modern period with its predominance of psychometrics and audiolingual methods, the use of L1 was not so evident and was regarded as belonging to the grammar-translation method in FLT. Lado (1967), however, did see some advantages in checking understanding in L1 in some cases. This use has become more accepted today for both listening (e.g. Boeijen, 1984) and reading comprehension (cf. e.g. Apelt, 1976; Desselmann and Hollmich, 1981), although it is not yet very frequent.

The use of translation into L1

To use translation into L1 systematically in the training of reading would lead to bad habit formation. Reading speed would slow down a lot and it cannot be guaranteed that the information is being processed. Translation is not a teaching method and should only be used when it is the most efficient way to explain word meaning or the occasional complicated structure. Keil (1979) sees complete translations into L1 as the most efficient way to control comprehension of non-literary texts, but he starts from the viewpoint of a beginner in a relatively unrelated target language. Belyayev wrote: 'Literal translation helps a great deal, not only to understand the text, but also to grasp the specific characteristics of thinking in a foreign language' (quoted Mooijman, 1983). Note that he is concerned with literal translation, not the translator's usual work. When no completely adequate translation is available because of lack of parallelism in the semantic fields, this ought to be indicated, to make the learners conscious of a problem that they might otherwise encounter only after a lot of FL-reading. Translation here means not the professional work, but a minimal transferring, conveying the meaning of the original text. A perfect style in L1 is not required.

A typology of errors in semantic processing has been developed by Ladmiral (explained by Konigs, 1984). He distinguishes on the one hand nonsensical translation (the worst error), inconsistent translation, due to lack of FL competence, and errors due to lack of L1 competence. These are all considered serious errors. On the other hand, errors and mistakes in L1 appear that are not taken very seriously as long as global text comprehension seems unimpeded. Even with such a typology the rating of a translation is not easily rendered objective and reliable.

The use of partial translation

To use translation only for certain structures or words, where the target group's decoding errors, such as interference, can be expected, solves some of the problems caused by translation as a testing procedure. The danger of translation becoming a habit decreases, for it is only used in cases where it would have been purposeful in the learning process. Translation works as a device for comprehension (control), not as a method. Testees who see the problem will not start to translate automatically without semantic processing, especially if they have been trained to use contextual guessing in cases where L1 does not help and command of the target language fails. The test consists of discrete comprehension items. This allows the calculation of reliabilities and the elimination of weak items, thereby measuring comprehension in a psycho-metrically more valid way than by a complete translation or by a summary. The test is moreover time-saving for both testee and rater.

Lado (1967) advises us 'to limit the use of translation techniques in foreign language tests to those problems that cannot be tested efficiently by other techniques' and gives another solution to the scoring problem. He suggests the provision of a translation in L1 with a blank left open for the specific problem using discrete-point items on separate sentences. This technique would be absurd for reading comprehension since the test would become an L1 cloze.

Item content

Part of the text of a reading comprehension test of German for Dutch-speakers, using partial translation, is given in the Appendix. The content of the test is highly related to the teaching method - a cognitive method using data from contrastive and error analysis (Hoogzand and

Lutjeharms, 1983). The test consists of two parts, from two to four very general questions on global text comprehension and about 20 items on detailed text comprehension requiring mainly short translations. These may be rather free, as long as the meaning is conveyed. The items deal with vocabulary problems like deceptive cognates or words lacking intra- or inter-lingual contrast (Lutjeharms, 1981), i.e. words that look easier than they are. Students are expected to know the most frequent words in their specialisation and the word families in this category. Items are either on vocabulary that has been dealt with or on text segments, where context helps in discovering and solving the problem. Some are on grammatical problems, mainly overlooked declension endings, such as reading a pre-positioned object as a subject, or confounding singular and plural nouns or article and relative pronoun. Part of a complex syntactic structure is sometimes used as well. Complex syntax only rarely causes errors because if a structure is not understood, attempts at comprehension are usually given up.

The test is based on a rather long LSP-text (about 160 newspaper lines) and so the language is presented in a holistic way. The purpose of the items, however, is to force the learner to solve specific linguistic problems. The items concentrate on the specific problems added to the reading process by the FL component. Because of this, the relevant context is often limited to the sentence or paragraph.

Limited use of a dictionary is allowed before receiving the question sheet, but only after a first global reading. The global reading is necessary to start the top-down processing, to concentrate attention on global meaning first. Otherwise, weak readers tend to focus on single words or problems connected with the assignment, even though they have been trained in the top-down procedure (Levenston, Nir and Blum-Kulka, 1984, made a comparable observation).

153

Part of the item content in fact measures learning achievement, testing lower-order skills like learned vocabulary and grammar and application of acquired rules and techniques. The intelligent reader can compensate for deficient linguistic processing by using higher-order skills like contextual guessing (by analysing word form or position in the sentence, by using the subject-matter of the text or sentence, by using text redundancy or internal consistency, scripts or schemes etc.). Some items involve both skills. Use of different kinds of processing, subskills and strategies varies enormously among testees (cf. van Krieken, 1982), as does the acquired degree of automisation. The test has proved to be very easy for students with near-native mastery of German, provided their mastery of Dutch (or English or French, which are allowed as alternatives) is as good or better. The translating activity seems not to disturb them and they are very fast at it.

An advantage of LSP texts is that the testees - if studying the same subject - are in a more or less equal position as far as the part played by extra-textual knowledge is concerned. This does not imply that they make equal use of it.

Item form

The whole of the testing part of the instrument, both the questions set and the answers required of the testees, is in L1. There are questions on both global and detailed text comprehension. The global comprehension questions are short answer items and there are only a few of them, as it is not possible to ask many. Because of this small number it is not possible to do item analysis on them.

Most of the detailed comprehension items are short translations with occasional questions on reference. These were item-analysed, to improve the reliability coefficients. Items on one single word or a question on a case (only used when it is essential for comprehension) have proved to have a low discrimination index and this happens independently of the difficulty of the item. The discrimination index is improved by adding some words to the item, even if these do not involve any extra difficulty. The low discrimination index could be caused by the very direct reference to the problem or by an inclination just to translate the single word or judge the case without contextualising it. The items are expressly constructed with an indication of the line and the first and last word(s) of the text segment to which they refer in order to encourage the testee to refer to the text before answering the item. Questions on references discriminate well (cf. item 3 in the Appendix). They are, of course, extremely relevant to the reading process and cannot be solved without reference to context. Items on frequent difficult words appear - as might be expected - to be very easy in target groups that have attended classes regularly. The low discrimination index may be due partly to lack of difficulty, but if context does not help at all, intelligent readers that have not attended classes tend to guess wrongly here (cf. item 4 in the Appendix: the wrong translation 'data' is possible in context).

Only very rarely does an item have to be eliminated from the scoring. An item can be bad because it allows equivocal answers or because of extra difficulty in the item not immediately apparent to the test constructor.

Results

For two tests, a multiple-choice (MC) version has been compared to the open-ended one. The first MC version consisted of four alternatives per item constructed by the teacher and corrected by colleagues. The MC version had lower reliability and proved to be easier. The correlation between course attendance and test result was higher for the open-ended version. The second MC version, again with four alternatives, was constructed with student answers from an open-ended version (N = 69; reliability by Cronbach's Alpha = 0.85). The most frequent errors were used as distractors and, if there was too little variety, errors made by testees with a high score were selected. For the open-ended version reliability was comparable to the first version (0.86, N = 39), but the MC version had very poor results (N = 34) and a reliability of 0.58. This would have risen to 0.66 if the worst item (-0.44) had been rejected. Again, the MC version was easier.

The testees were asked to indicate for the MC version whether they would have found the answer without the alternatives, whether these had helped them, or whether they had guessed. For 680 possibilities (N = 34 X 20 items) 312 items had been correctly answered without help from the answers provided and 130 wrongly, 92 items had been correctly answered with help from the information contained in the alternatives and 50 wrongly, whereas guessing was 30 times right and 48 times wrong. In three cases, no solution was indicated. This shows that guessing is not so important. Most of the guessing occurred on the item with 0.44 discrimination index (11 times wrong, three right), on a problem not dealt with in all groups and hence unsuitable. The three items with a negative discrimination index were those where most of the guessing had occurred, in one case 11 times correctly.

Reliability coefficients and correlations with other parts of the examination

Reliability coefficients for the detailed comprehension test part are quite satisfactory for a non-standardised test, between 0.80 and 0.90. Classical test theory has been used up to now since inter-item independency can in general be assumed, most items being solvable on a paragraph or sentence level. There might still be a problem, since the whole text content often helps as well, but this has not yet been investigated.

Correlations (Pearson) between global and detailed text comprehension are low (0.39 to 0.59), as was expected. Attendance in class does influence the score for detailed text comprehension, which relies mainly on the FL component of the reading skill, whereas the global text comprehension items deal rather with general reading skills. The detailed comprehension test correlates higher (0.44 to 0.73) on the grammar test, consisting of questions on the same text but asked in such a way that an indicated structure has to be changed, mostly into another case. This has to be trained and depends highly on learning. This last factor might equally explain the more or less high correlations with the oral proficiency test, a classic interview with two raters and required only for some groups.

Conclusions

This test form proved to be suitable as a testing procedure for the target groups. From the point of view of test construction the main problem lies in the choice of text. The text has to present varied difficulties in grammar and vocabulary for the target group. Test construction itself is then easy. Scoring is fast for open-ended items, as all answers are short and the solution(s) known beforehand. The test is therefore objective. Reliability has been improved by item analysis and is quite satisfactory. Validity is the main problem. Content validity is accounted for in the construction, by relying on examinee characteristics, learning history and test purpose (cf. Stevenson, 1981), but real validation studies have not yet been carried out.

Acknowledgement

I should like to thank my colleague Frank Winter for reading through the English text.

References

Apelt, W. (1976) Positionen und Probleme der Fremdsprachenpsychologie. Halle (Saale): VEB Max Niemeyer Verlag.

Beaugrande, R. de (1981) Design criteria for process models of reading. Reading Research Quarterly, 16, 261-315.

Boeijen, M. (1984) Testing listening comprehension: notions and functions as 'discrete points' in a communicative context. In T. Culhane, C. Klein-Braley and D.K. Stevenson (Eds.) Practice and Problems in Language Testing. Colchester: University of Essex Department of Language and Linguistics Occasional paper no. 26 76-89.

Davies, N.F. (Ed.) (1983) Theme issue: the receptive way. System, 11, 244-323.

Desselmann, G. and Hellmich H. (Autorenkollektiv unter Leutung von) (1981) Didaktik des Fremdsprachenunterricht, Deutsch als Fremdsprache. Leipzig: VEB Verlag Enzyklopadie.

Hoogzand, A. and Lutjeharms, M. (1983) Die entwicklung rezeptiver Sprachfertigkeiten bei Betriebswirtschaftsstudenten: Biespiele aus der unterrichtspraxis. In P. De Cuyper, M.J. De Vriendt and M. Urbain (Eds.) Fremdsprachen in Wirtschaft und Technik. Mons: Universite de l'Etat, 89-104.

Juhasz, J. (1970) Probleme der Interferenz. Budapest: Akademiai Kiado.

Keil, R.D. (1979) Die Ubersetzung im Russischunterricht. Kongressbericht der 9. Jahrestagung der Gesellschaft fur Angewandte Linguistik, GAL e.V., Mainz 1978. IRAL-Sonderband, Band 1: Sprachlern -und lehrmaterialien. Heidelberg: Julius Groos Verlag, 229-233.

Konigs, F.G. (1984) Zentrale Begriffe aus der Wissenschaftlichen Beschaftigung mit Ubersetzen (Teil 5). Ubersetzung und Fremdsprachenunterricht. Lebende Sprachen, 29, 153-156.

Krieken, R. van. (1982) Vertalen en begrijpen. Toegepaste Taalwetenschap in Artikelen, 13, 128-147.

Lado, R. (1967) Language Testing. London: Longmans.

Levenston, E.A., Nir, R. and Blum-Kulka, S. (1984) Discourse analysis and the testing of reading comprehension by cloze techniques. In A.K. Pugh and J.M. Ulijn (Eds.) Reading for Professional Purposes. London: Heinemann, 202-212.

Lutjeharms, M. (1981) Zum Testen des fachorientierten Leseverstandnisses: ein Beispiel. In T. Culhane, C. Klein-Braley and D.K. Stevenson (Eds.) Practice and Problems in Language Testing. Colchester: University of Essex Department of Language and Linguistics Occasional paper no. 26 88-94.

Mooijam, J.P. (1983) I spy. In search of meaning. In search, too, of a European school programme of modern foreign language learning. System, 11, 255-269.

Nord, J.R. (1980) Developing listening fluency before speaking: an alternative paradigm. System, 8, 1-22.

Parreren, C.F. van, and Schouten-van Parreren, M.C. (1981) Contextual guessing : a trainable reader strategy. System, 9, 235-241.

Schouten-van Parreren, M.C. (1983) Wisseling van de wacht in de vreemde-talendidactiek. Levende Talen, 378, 22-29.

Smelcer, P.A., Patwardhan, N., Wilson, A. and
Raffler-Engel, W. von (1980) Linguistic
awareness of the translation process. System, 8,
59-70.

Stevenson, D.K. (1981) All of the above: on
problems in the testing of FL reading. System, 9,
267-273.

Voss, B. (1984) Slips of the Ear: investigations
into the speech perception behaviour of German
speakers of English. Tubingen: Gunter Narr
Verlag.

Appendix

1. Extract of text (about 1/4 of full article)

Denn die deutsche Anleihe sollte ausschliesslich
helfen, die Anpassung an den strukturellen Wandel
der Wirtschaft zu vollsiehen. In ihrem bulletin
vom 10. April, 1981 schrieb die Bundesregierung,
'dass eine kurzfristige Stimulierung der
Nachfrage durch zusatzliche offentliche
Ausgabenprogramme nicht geeignet ist, einen
wirksamen Beitrag zur Losung er Strukturprobleme
der deutschen Wirtschaft zu leisten'. Weil die
Regierung vor allem mittelstandischen Betrieben
unter die Arme greifen wollte, begrenzte sie die
Hochstsumme der uber die Anleihe finanzierten
Kredite auf acht Millionen Mark je Unternehmen.
Der finanzielle Beitrag des Bundes erschopfte
sich in der Verbilligung der Kredite um etwa 2,25
Prozentpunkten gegenuber dem marktzins ... Auch
wenn die Umfrage sich vor allem nach
Investitionen zur Energie-einsparung erkund-
igte, sieht IHK-Geschaftsfuhrer Wilfried
Naujocks keinen Grund, an den Ergebnissen zu
zweifeln: 'Wir bleiben bei unserer Feststellung.' Und diese heisst eindeutig, dass mit
dem Programm uberwiegend Mitnehmereffekte
provoziert worden sind und dass fur die
ursprunglich wichtigsten Ziele Energieeinsparen
und Olsubstitution nur elf beziehungsweise drei

Prozent der bisher behwilligten kredite ausgegeben worden sind.

Dass die Kredite bei der KfW zugig abfliessen, kann weder uberraschen noch als Indiz fur Erfolg heralten. Denn jede Ware - auch ein Kredit - findet leicht Kaufer, wenn sie unter Preis angeboten wird. Fur die Unternehmen ist es unerdies ein beinahe risiko loses Geschaft. Wenn die Markzinsen unter vier oder acht Jahre festgeschriebenen Zinsen fur die KfW-Kredite absinken, konnen die Firmen vorzeitig aussteigen. Der Steuerzahler mag sich angesechts der mageren Bilanz damit trosten, dass ihn das Programm keineswegs 6, 3 Milliarden Mark kosten wird, wie der Name suggeriert.

(P. Christ, Geld weg, Ziel verfehlt.
Nur wenige zusatzliche Investitionen durch billige Darlehen. Die Zeit, 15.1.82; reproduced by permission of the publisher).

2. Some items (total number: 20)

Difficulty Discrimination

Difficulty	Discrimination	
0.80	0.42	1 & 2. line 3-5: translate from 'dass eine... (to) ... geeignet ist'.
0.50	0.77	Problems: long postpositioned attribute and in question 2, vocabulary problems: zusatzlich (lack of contrast), offentlich (deceptive cognate.)
0.56	0.75	3. line 8: 'der' belongs to what word? What is the case?

0.92	0.24	4. line 14: Translate 'an den Ergebnissen su zweifeln'. Problem: ergebnisse (deceptive cognate.)
0.60	0.76	5. line 16: What does 'Mitnehmereffekte' mean?
0.85	0.83	6. line 20-21: Translate from 'kann weder ... (to) ... herhalten'. Problems: 'weder' and 'erfolg' (deceptive cognates). The meaning of 'herhalten' was given beforehand, as it was not in the dictionary, nor seen in class.
0.71	0.37	7. line 26: translate from 'Der Steursah- ler ... (to) damit trosten'. Problems: meaning of 'mag' and 'angesichts'.

Reliability by Cronbach's Alpha = 0.9; N=23.

The Misuse of Reading Tests: malfunctioning technicians or a function of the technology?

Barry Stierer

One of the interesting findings to emerge from the Evaluation of Testing in Schools Project (cf. Gipps and Goldstein, 1983; Gipps et al., 1983) at the London Institute of Education was the ambivalence with which many educationalists approach educational testing in general, and the testing of reading in particular. Most people we interviewed, from the academics, researchers and HMIs involved in the work of the Assessment of Performance Unit, to the local authority officers, advisers and psychologists responsible for county and borough testing schemes, to head teachers and classroom teachers, were attracted and at the same time put off by the business of testing. This leads me to suggest that there is an implicit debate going on about the suitability of standardised reading tests as measures of reading competence, and that that debate encapsulates many important issues pertaining to the teaching and learning of reading - curriculum issues, pedagogical issues and social and political issues. My aim in this paper is to explore some of the arguments in this debate. I use the word 'explore' deliberately, since my ideas are tentative and are intended to spark more informed discussion rather than to inter reading tests for all time. The paper is exploratory in the additional sense that I intend to point out the weaknesses inherent in some of the arguments against the use of reading tests, as well as in the counter arguments offered by the tests' constructors, users and apologists.

The debate

Critics of reading tests rally round one or more of the following three battle cries:

1. Most reading tests are out of date.
The tests which most teachers have access to, or are required to administer, are generally at least ten years old and often much older. Norms become outdated and misleading, vocabulary and language structures become stilted and off-putting, and as Goodacre (1979) has pointed out, models of reading and reading acquisition change over time, rendering the models built into the tests obsolete.

2. Reading tests give little or no diagnostic information.
The tests which most teachers have access to, or are required to administer, provide little more than a single figure for 'reading'. This figure may indicate how well a group performs relative to a larger sample, or relative to each other, or how well an individual performs relative to a past performance on the same test. However, it does not enable a greater understanding of an individual as a reader: his or her strengths and weaknesses, strategies and responses, attitudes and habits.

3. Reading tests do not measure 'real reading'.
Critics point out that the reading demands of standardised reading tests are considerably different from the reading demands which children encounter in and out of school, and therefore produce a distorted picture of their reading ability. 'Real' reading, the critics argue, is a complex thinking process which will vary in its effectiveness from context to context according to the reader's need to read, the content and structure of the text, and the reader's background knowledge and interests. A child's successful performance on a reading test does not depend on these vital aspects of the reading

skill, any more than a child's poor performance indicates a weakness as a reader in the fullest sense.

The psychometric 'industry' has a number of defences against this kind of criticism. In response to the charge that the tests are out of date, it is possible to answer that the 'industry' cannot accept responsibility for the use of outdated tests. Newer tests are available, based on more up-to-date standardisations and reading models, and the industry promotes the use of these tests over older ones. Other papers in this volume demonstrate the continuing efforts being made to produce modern instruments.

A similar defence can be offered in response to the complaint that the tests provide little or no diagnostic information. Tests produced in recent years do generate profiles which enable a greater understanding of an individual reader. In fact, it has been argued by some that the sophistication of diagnostic information generated by some reading tests now exceeds that of many teachers' own understanding of the reading process. It can also be said that there is **some** diagnostic information available from even the most rudimentary reading test if one is sensitive to it. Again, the testing industry cannot be held responsible if their newer, more diagnostic instruments are not widely used or if test users do not make use of the diagnostic information provided by whatever tests they use.

The psychometric response to the third charge, that the tests do not measure 'real' reading, is a more elaborate one. First, it would be pointed out that reading tests are not always what they seem. What appears on the surface to be a narrow and artificial reading experience may merely 'stand for' the more complex process, which the test constructors have demonstrated through a stat-istical validation procedure. Critics who fail to appreciate the intricacies of reading test validity theory appear to have a temperamental aversion to all things statistical and can therefore easily be dismissed.

Second, psychometricians would point out that reading tests are not designed to measure reading in its very fullest sense. The tests are, by admission, blunt instruments which are only capable of measuring a limited range of reading skills. To a test user who is aware of the test's limitations, useful information is provided. However, the industry cannot take responsibility for a user's exaggerated interpretation of test data.

So the critics of reading tests are right on one level, but their criticisms fall well short of the comprehensive indictment they claim to be. I'd like to look again at my simulated defence of reading tests, and to try and extract from it certain implicit principles which would appear to inform the thinking of those who support the use of the tests.

1. Reading tests are imperfect.
They are limited in what they measure and in the kind of information they provide. They are prone to a degree of error and they are impermanent. If tests are limited in the aspects of reading they measure, it follows that it is technically possible to conceptualise reading as a collection of subskills and to assess one or more of these subskills without making claims to test the global competence. A view of reading as a unified process, in which many diverse and interdependent skills are called into play for every reading act, is therefore incompatible with the principles of reading test theory.

2. Reading tests are greatly improvable.
Other chapters in this volume testify to the widespread belief that we are not bound to tolerate the weaknesses of existing tests. Tests' imperfections are predominantly technical, how-

ever, since reading tests are becoming better all the time. Most obstacles to much better tests are surmountable technical ones.

3. Reading tests are, at least potentially, valid.
Despite its pervasive status as a hidden cognitive process, reading is considered to be potentially accessible by means of observing certain kinds of outcomes or behaviours under certain kinds of conditions. It is, therefore, at least technically possible to generalise about some construct of reading competence from the outcome of a relatively short, impersonal and contrived reading experience.

4. Reading tests are neutral with respect to their use.
Reading tests cannot in themselves be misleading or damaging. They are only misleading or damaging when they are used incorrectly. For competent and well-informed users, fully aware of the tests' limitations, reading tests are an important part of the assessment process. Many advocates of reading tests bemoan the allegedly widespread 'misuse' of reading tests, and adopt the posture of the teachers' champion by exhorting the profession to 'improve its ability to use tests effectively' (Pumfrey, 1977), rather than by discouraging the use of tests altogether.

Examples of 'misuse'

I should like to scrutinise this last principle, since I think it is here that some of the contradictions and underlying values inherent in the tests can be found. I shall briefly review several instances where reading tests have been used in ways which the tests' advocates might regard as 'incorrect', and I shall be asking how completely we can separate these examples of 'misuse' from the technology itself. Each example highlights the use of reading tests at a different level of the education system, and came to light as a result of our investigation into the uses of standardised testing on the Evaluation of Testing in Schools Project.

The first example relates to the work of the Assessment of Performance Unit (APU), and in particular to the way in which the APU's Language Monitoring Team made use of the National Survey Form 6 reading test (NS6) in its early monitoring exercises. The establishment of a Language Monitoring Team at the NFER in the mid-1970s aroused anxieties among many educationalists about 'backwash' effects on reading and language teaching in schools, and about moves to control language and literacy curricula from the centre of the system. However, assurances were made that the Team was developing qualitatively different instruments from those previously used. These were to be based on new principles of test construction and on a more comprehensive model of language use, giving rise to results with new meanings. The expressed aim of the Team was to devise instruments which would replace the old NS6 (the reading test which had been used in regular national reading surveys since 1955), whose weaknesses and inadequacies were repeatedly emphasised.

Rosen (1982) has examined the uses made of the NS6 in the first primary survey conducted by the Language Monitoring Team. He points out that, having laid bare the inadequacy of NS6, the Team somewhat surprisingly administered it to a subsample of children in the 1979 survey of eleven-year-olds. The APU then carried out two comparisons. First, they compared their 1979 results using NS6 with those obtained by the HMI primary survey in 1976/77 using the same test (Department of Education and Science, 1978). APU concluded that no significant differences between the two sets of scores were revealed. No reason for this comparison was given beyond the assertion that 'it is desirable' to establish 'a link with previous surveys' (APU, 1981).

The Team went further. By means of statistical manipulation the Team compared their 1979 results using the NS6 with the performance by the same children on the APU's own reading tests. The criterion-referenced profiles of competence generated by the APU tests, allegedly reflecting a comprehensive view of the reading process, were correlated with the single norm-referenced figures generated by the NS6 and a correlation coefficient of 0.77 was achieved. It would appear that performance on the new tests can be summarised in a single global score for 'reading' and then compared with scores on a conceptually different test. Rosen asks 'What has been the whole point of the APU's testing of reading in an entirely new way?' (1982, p.22). It seems that, after all, the only real weakness of NS6 is that it lacks 'face validity', if it can be reliably correlated with a more comprehensive battery of tests. If the APU's exercise constitutes, in effect, a new demonstration of NS6's construct validity with reference to a more comprehensive reading model, can the NS6 now be used more confidently as a measure of 'real reading'?

The second example is taken from the findings from our survey of testing policies and practices in local education authorities (LEAs), carried out in 1980 and 1981. We discovered that, in many LEAs, a single reading test was being used for diverse purposes, including the monitoring of standards over time, the allocation of resources, facilitation of transfer from primary to secondary school, and the identification of children in need of special teaching. It is not unusual for schools to duplicate the testing for transfer and screening carried out by their own LEAs. In several cases, we found that, in addition to these managerial purposes, local authorities encouraged classroom teachers to make use of the scores derived from the reading surveys in their own evaluations. However, the tests used by these LEAs were almost invariably not designed for the multitude of purposes for which they were used. The manual for one of the more frequently used tests in LEA surveys of seven- and eight-year-olds, the NFER Reading Test A, states explicitly that the test is designed for large populations and is not suitable for individual assessment and diagnosis. Nevertheless, LEAs did not point out the limitations of the test to classroom teachers; indeed there was an implicit pressure to take the results of the test into serious account.

Finally, we found through interviews and case studies of teachers' attitudes and practices with respect to testing that examples of 'incorrect' uses of reading tests abound. We found many teachers expressing a preference for oral word recognition tests over newer tests requiring a written response, and a large number of these teachers were using the results from such tests as if they were indices of a much more comprehensive competence than oral word recognition. We found teachers exercising considerable selectivity in the test scores they 'took seriously' and those they ignored. We found some teachers using test scores as the basis for critical decisions of organisation, such as the setting of classroom reading groups and the identification of children for special remedial teaching, even when the tests used were explicitly not designed to enable that kind of small-scale decision-making. We found some teachers administering and marking reading tests in unorthodox ways. And we found some teachers 'reading into' some single-figure test scores elaborate diagnoses of individual pupils' teaching needs, such as the need for more training in phonic decoding skills, the need for more group reading work, the need to play more 'reading games', and the need to progress through the reading scheme by means of oral reading to a teacher rather than by means of independent silent reading.

Can we dismiss these examples as failures to appreciate the expressed limitations of reading test technology, or do they begin to cast a shadow over the technology itself? I should like to suggest as a suitable topic for further discussion, investigation and thought, the proposition that it is impossible ultimately to separate the principles underlying the construction and advocacy of the tests from these and other instances of reading test 'misuse'.

Social context of reading test 'misuse'

To support this proposition, I would point out first that the social context of each instance of 'misuse' must be taken fully into account. In the case of the APU's use of the NS6, for example, we cannot separate the Language Monitoring Team's comparability exercises from the tremendous constraints under which they worked. Despite the opportunity they had to carry out an independent research investigation into the kinds of literacy children are able to use, or into the nature and underlying causes of under-achievement in language skill among school pupils (both part of early APU briefs), the Team was under considerable pressure from the politicians and officials at the Department of Education and Science to enable comprehensible pronouncements on the trend in reading standards over time to be made. This pressure can be traced back to a more general alarm over the efficiency of the education system and to greater calls for quantifiable measures of educational 'output'. As Rosen puts it, 'the inescapable conclusion is that the paymasters have called the tune, possibly against the better judgement of the research team' (1982, p.21).

Local authority officers, advisers and psychologists also work under strong and sometimes conflicting pressures. They must satisfy the demands of education committees which may not always give priority to educational objectives. The increasing use by LEAs of private firms of accountants and systems analysts as evaluators of cost efficiency highlights the sense of compromise which many LEA staff currently feel. They find themselves increasingly in need of narrow indices of educational 'output' in order to identify the priorities of the service, and yet they must appear to allocate steadily dwindling resources fairly and effectively. All this may not rest easily with their abiding professional commitment to good educational practice in schools, colleges, clinics and so on.

And in schools, heads and classroom teachers are continually taking important decisions which require a wide range of information about the reading competence of pupils. Heads in our survey reported their need for some form of 'external calibration' by which to judge their own school's achievement in relation to other schools. They often require an impersonal focus when discussing pupils with teachers and parents. And increasingly, they need persuasive evidence when 'making a case' for additional resources for the school. A list of teachers' needs for information about pupils' reading competence might include the following.

1. They need to identify children in need of special teaching at a time when need may be found to exceed provision.

2. They need to match individual children to suitable texts and tasks even though time for sensitive observation is at a premium.

3. They need to meet the 'special needs' of E2L, multi-lingual and handicapped children when all that may be available is traditional 'remedial' teaching.

172

4.   They need general feedback on teaching and learning.

5.   They need frequent catalysts for action.

6.   They will soon need to satisfy new teacher appraisal criteria.

7.   They need evidence to support controversial practices or special requests.

8.   They need to meet high professional standards with diminishing resources available for replacing outdated materials or for in-service education and training.

I have tried here to outline some aspects of the social context in which reading tests are used. I suggest two things at this point in relation to this social context. First, I suggest that the promotion of reading tests as suitable measures of reading competence, however cautious, cannot be abstracted from the real world in which that advice might be taken. A technology which is, on the one hand, limited in what it can measure but which, on the other hand, holds out the promise of valid, comprehensive and context-independent information about a reader's competence invites the kinds of 'misuses' I described earlier in the far from idealised settings where tests are used. Similarly, tests which, by definition, soon go out of date and need replacing cannot easily be abstracted from the impoverished educational world in which they are used.

Secondly, and conversely, I suggest that the constructors and advocates of reading tests are partly responsible for (inadvertently) creating some of the contradictory and over-simplified needs for information which give rise to 'misuse' of the tests. Reading tests are the product of a technology which, for example, claims the power to enable comparisons of reading 'standards' over

time and across varied populations, and which
appears capable of measuring narrow skills in a
brief and artificial context and then general-
ising, on the basis of that performance, about a
wider competence in a wider range of contexts.
These claims have contributed significantly to a
contradictory state of affairs. The respectability and scientific prestige of the tests are
sustained, while at the same time needs for
information are engendered which increasingly
outstrip the current limitations of the
technology itself. In this sense reading tests
may function to create the need for further
testing of reading.

Would our resources and energies be more
productively deployed by developing and
promoting assessment techniques for reading
which meet the real educational needs of real
teachers and children in real classrooms, rather
than by promoting a technology which appears to
satisfy needs which are in part artifacts
themselves?

Interpretation and science

Following on from this observation about the
inseparability of reading tests from the social
context of their use (or 'misuse'), it is vital to
consider as well the nature of interpretation as
it relates to scores derived from reading tests.
Many examples of 'misuse' centre on the
interpretation (or 'misinterpretation') of test
results by teachers and others. In my own study of
classroom reading assessment (Stierer, 1983),
for example, I found that the same score on the
same test can carry very different meanings about
readers' competence and needs for the same
teacher. And similar scores on the same test
suggested different teaching strategies for
different teachers, depending on their own views
about reading and about teaching and learning
generally.

In a fascinating study, Leiter (1976) examined teachers' use of background knowledge to interpret test scores. He points out that one of the reasons for the use of standardised tests is to eliminate the teacher's use of subjective knowledge when assessing their pupils. And yet, Leiter found that, in order to render test scores meaningful, teachers invariably embedded the scores in just the kinds of knowledge the scores are supposed to replace. The professional judgement needed by teachers to 'make sense' of their pupils' test scores consisted of 'using background knowledge to form a context for interpreting the scores' (p.41). That background knowledge comprised details about, for example, pupils' home backgrounds, pupils' classroom behaviour, and views about curriculum, pedagogy and learning. Teachers' experience of administering and marking the test, and their understanding of the particular test, were also invoked when accounting for the meanings given to test scores. Teachers' relationships with their pupils also helped to shape the precise meanings they ascribed to their pupils' scores. Teachers' use of that background knowledge was found, moreover, to be both heterogeneous (i.e. different kinds of knowledge were used in the interpretation of different pupils' scores) and situation-specific (i.e. the same kinds of knowledge were sometimes used to derive different kinds of meanings from different pupils' scores).

Leiter's conclusions were far from judgemental in respect of teachers. Rather than upbraid teachers for their subjective approach, and entreat them to be more 'scientific', Leiter suggests that the use of subjective knowledge is the only possible way in which sense can be made of 'objective' test scores. Indeed he asserts that it is this subjectivity that gives the test scores their objective and factual status:

Numbers have an equivocal sense when they are simply presented to somebody. It is only when they are provided with a scenic source that they begin to take on meaning. The use of background knowledge not only provides the numbers with their specific sense, it is in and through the use of background knowledge that their "objective" character is accomplished ... Because the test scores are potentially equivocal, background knowledge is used to resolve that equivocality and thereby provide the scores with their factual properties. While sociologists and educators imply that the use of background knowledge undermines the objectivity of the test, I have shown that it is through the use of background knowledge that the objectivity of the test is secured by rendering an otherwise truncated account of the student's capabilities into a rich and immediate context of tacitly and explicitly known matters. (pp. 64-65)

Leiter's analysis should be considered seriously by anyone promoting the use of reading tests as 'objective' measures of pupils' reading competence. Test scores, in and of themselves, are not meaningful. They must be rendered meaningful using knowledge and information derived from sources outside the test itself. In agreeing with Leiter's argument I am not suggesting that the use of background knowledge to interpret test scores is simply a weakness of human nature which can be guarded against. I am suggesting that the recourse to an elaborate social, professional and subjective context is intrinsic to every act of making sense of numerical information, however 'scientific' the particular circumstances may be. There is therefore a real sense in which the promotion of numbers as indices of readers' competence actually invites and authorises subjectivity in a way which less quantifiable assessment measures may go some way towards preventing. By recommending assessment techniques which require their users to go outside the techniques themselves for the information which makes them intelligible, the advocates of reading tests may inadvertenty be encouraging judgements and evaluations which draw upon information which is far from reading-specific, and in so doing perform a disservice to teachers and pupils alike.

This relates back to my earlier point about the pressures under which teachers work. The current atmosphere is one in which many teachers are required to administer reading tests, or feel that reading tests should be used, and one in which teachers feel that scores should be taken into account. As I have said, the psychometric industry must take some responsibility for this atmosphere. In such an atmosphere, test users will inevitably feel that there is meaning to be derived from test scores, and will be encouraged implicitly to engage in the kind of subjectivity which is intrinsic to the interpretation of numbers.

It seems that, on the basis of this analysis, educationalists are faced with an important choice. We can make it absolutely clear, whenever we promote reading tests, that the interpretation of test scores is an inherently subjective process. But is it not possible that the scarce resources currently available to the education service would be better deployed in the development and dissemination of processes for reading assessment which are perhaps more explicitly interpretive but less 'equivocal' (to use Leiter's term)? Building upon teachers' existing expertise and knowledge, rather than intensifying pressures to adopt a spurious scientism, may be a more appropriate and effective approach to improving the quality of literacy teaching.

Acknowlegement

(The author wishes to thank Dr. Caroline Gipps for her comments on earlier drafts of this chapter.)

References

APU (1981) Language Performance in Schools: Primary Survey No. 1. London: HMSO.

Department of Education and Science (1978) Primary Education in England: a Survey by HM Inspectors. London: HMSO.

Gipps, C.V. and Goldstein, H. (1983) Monitoring Children. London: Heinemann Educational Books.

Gipps, C.V., Steadman, S.D., Blackstone, T.V. and Stierer, B.M. (1983) Testing Children: standardised testing in local education authorities and schools. London: Heinemann Educational Books.

Goodacre, E. (1979) What is reading: which model? In M.St.J. Raggett, C. Tutt and P. Raggett (Eds.) Assessment and Testing of Reading. London: Ward Lock Educational.

Leiter, K.W. (1976) Teachers' use of background knowledge to interpret test scores. Sociology of Education, 49, 59-65.

Pumfrey, P.D. (1977) Reading measurement and evaluation: some current concerns and promising developments. In J. Gilliland (Ed.) Reading: research and classroom practice. London: Ward Lock Educational.

Rosen, H. (1982) The Language Monitors. (Bedford Way Papers No. 11). London: Institute of Education, University of London.

Stierer, B.M. (1983) Reading tests in the classroom: a case study. Paper presented to the Symposium on Testing and Assessment at the Annual Conference of the British Educational Research Association, London.